BUSINESS IS THE PEOPLE & PEOPLE ARE THE BUSINESS

BUSINESS IS THE PEOPLE & PEOPLE ARE THE BUSINESS

BREAK ONE AND THE OTHER WILL BREAK,

HOW ETHICS AND ETIQUETTE

PROTECT BOTH

VAHÉ AKAY

iUniverse, Inc.

New York Lincoln Shanghai

Business is the People & People are the Business
Break one and the other will break,
How ethics and etiquette protect both

Copyright © 2006 by Vahé Akay

iUniverse books may be ordered through booksellers or by contacting:

iUniverse
2021 Pine Lake Road, Suite 100
Lincoln, NE 68512
www.iuniverse.com
1-800-Authors (1-800-288-4677)

TXU1268403

ISBN-13: 978-0-595-38297-2 (pbk)
ISBN-13: 978-0-595-82668-1 (ebk)
ISBN-10: 0-595-38297-5 (pbk)
ISBN-10: 0-595-82668-7 (ebk)

Printed in the United States of America

Acknowledgments

It would not have been possible to create this book without the encouragement, and the support I received from Susan Adams and Rick Price, who believed in my character and my ability to address a topic as critical for our current times as this.

I would also like to recognize the individual from whom I learned, directly and indirectly, what is right and what is wrong for all aspects of business, my father, Apraham Akay.

My father's influence on my development and evolution was most significant, during and after his life. I learned from my father's high ethical standards, discipline, respect for all living things, tremendous accomplishments, perseverance, and his love and care for people, for life, and all living things in general. I learned that it is never too late to achieve success in any environment. Of the many strengths of my father's character, two stand out for me:

- He never complained despite all the difficulties and tragedies he encountered during his long life!

- He refused to gossip about people. He didn't even attack people he disagreed with or whom he openly recognized as having done horrible deeds. Instead he would give his points of view about their acts and what he would do or would have done if he were in their place. He would only do so if he were asked for his opinion. He was never the instigator.

I never once witnessed or heard him complain or gossip. He took the good with the bad and made the best of it. My father, however, was not without flaws. Just like any human being, he made mistakes, and I learned from them as well.

I am still learning from my memories of my father and will be doing so for the rest of my life.

Contents

It Has Been Proven That a Tree

Gently Touched and Growing Near

Soothing Music Manifests More

Complete Health Than a Tree

Growing Alone Near Harsh Noises

Introduction

Life Is Lived Through Choices and Decisions

In December of 2001, I became unemployed after twenty-two years in the high-tech industry. I was laid off from a semiconductor company where I was the vice president of marketing and an officer of the company.

For more than a year, I spent an average of six hours a day on the phone and on the computer looking for a new career opportunity. I signed up on executive search Web sites, visited target company Web sites, and sent hundreds of emails to hiring managers. I talked to many hiring managers, recruiters, colleagues, and friends in the high-tech industry and other fields. I even tried to start my own company but had no success. I began wondering if I had reached the end of my career. (Granted, the economy was in the tank, the job market was terrible, unemployment was high—but still, this was bad, really bad.)

It was at that time that I realized that the culture of the high-tech industry had drastically changed. The decision makers, people at the top with whom I had been speaking regarding new career opportunities, had developed a myopic vision and view of people, their capabilities, and their qualifications. Although they looked at my resume, asked questions, gave feedback, and made comments about it and my job search in general, they paid little attention to what I was saying as I explained relevant details not included in the resume. And these details were important. I described the career decisions I had had to make and why I made them. I reluctantly shared personal events, even those over which I had no control, to shed light on some of my decisions and career changes. But nothing seemed to register with anyone.

At first I thought it was me. I thought my explanations were not clear enough, or maybe I wasn't good enough for the positions I was applying for. But after a year of trying to find a new job, it became clear to me that the explanation was to be found in the way businesses were managed and conducted. More accurately, it was the way people in those businesses were being groomed, trained, and managed to run the business and make decisions.

That was a moment of clarity for me. I reflected on my many years in the high-tech industry working for several large and small companies, public as well as startups, in various capacities. As a witness to the conduct of personnel at all levels of the organization, I remembered how surprised I had been at times at the way people treated one another, what the outcomes of the treatment were, and how they affected everyone throughout the organization. The effects were felt not only during work hours but also outside of work. Other individuals also have witnessed unethical conduct and have tried to write business books based on their observations and desire to correct the situation. However, what was missing from the business books I'd studied during my school years and my career was the identification and recognition of the most important component for any business entity: its people, the human component of business, the employees of the business entity. To succeed is all about the proper way of human interaction and the treatment of the human component of business. This component, of course, is the people who will carry out and perform all the business activities and strive to achieve the goals of the business entity. The mind and the body of the employee are what will carry this burden and deliver the desired business results. When the individual is broken, so is the business. Therefore, the concept that "business is the people & people are the business" is true; if you break one, you will most certainly break the other!

It is, therefore, crucial for any business entity to ensure that its people are intact, for they will lead the business to success, or to failure for that matter. For the impact of the human factor to be powerful, productive, and positive, all employees must be ethical and follow the proper etiquette in conducting themselves and their business. The dictionary defines the word "ethic" as "a system of moral principles or values." It also defines ethic as "a principle of right or good behavior," so the principles in the first definition must be right and good. Furthermore, the definition of ethics goes on to describe it as "the specific moral choices an individual makes in relating to others." This captures the essence of the word "ethics."

The definition continues by stating that the word "ethics" outlines the rules or standards of conduct governing the members of a profession. This highlights the importance of ethics to professional life and defines what needs to be understood and practiced without any conditions. Ethics consist of a set of moral choices we make in relating to others, to the people of a business.

The word "etiquette" is defined as "the forms and practices prescribed by social convention or by authority." So, it is not sufficient to only do the right and moral thing; it is important to do it the right way, the socially or professionally acceptable way. We do not live alone, in our own individual worlds, in a cocoon. We live with others, among people of many colors, beliefs, backgrounds, cultures, and religions to name just a few of the differences. To create synergy and harmony, we must follow certain rules of conduct. During certain phases of our lives, we may find a rule or social custom not agreeable to us and not in line with our opinions. However, many of these rules of conduct have been in existence for many years, decades, even centuries, and have passed the test of time. They have been proven to be valuable, useful, and correct. It is, therefore, prudent of us to exercise patience before judging or ignoring these rules. We should give these rules a chance by allowing ourselves to practice, apply, exercise, and use some of them before making our final decision and passing judgment. The results of doing so have been satisfying and positive to many people, including me, in their personal as well as their professional lives.

I am neither a practicing psychologist nor a sociologist, and I do not have a degree in either field. However, I am a person with significant life experiences. These experiences taught me, at a young age, quite a bit about people and their traits and behaviors in different environments and situations. I am also someone whose experiences, good and bad, have taught him much about the impact of human behavior, the human factor, on personal as well as on professional life. This book, however, will present the dynamics of conducting business through the human component of business, the people of the business, its personnel.

As the saying goes, "It's all about people…" People are the most powerful creatures on the planet because of the ability to think, and to have emotions and character. Countries are built and torn down by people. People create machines that can fly, submerge, or float. However, even the most powerful and smartest of these machines, including computers, are just dumb heaps of metal and plastics without people operating them.

This book is intended as a vehicle to help the individuals who manage organizations and businesses reach out to their employees and take care of them, treating them with respect, honesty, fairness, and dignity. We all have heard company executives use the phrase "Our most valuable asset is our employees." If that is so, then they must prove it, demonstrate it, and live by it.

It is true that employees are the most valuable assets of any business. Companies have an obligation not only to themselves, but also to society as a whole. Employees spend more time a day at work than anywhere else. If their work environment is unhealthy, then they will become unhealthy. This will affect the employees' lives outside the workplace, eventually spilling over into the rest of society and acting as an avalanche, crushing everything in its path—the family, the economy, and the entire health of a country.

The intent of this book is to point out to decision makers, whether supervisors, managers, directors, vice presidents or CEOs, that their decisions cannot focus on the bottom line alone and at all times. The point from which to start the process of caring for the business to facilitate and achieve its success must be attention to its people, the employees, every single one of them, and not just the bottom line. It is the people of the business entity who will make the bottom-line numbers what they are intended to be—profitable and growing. The way to accomplish this success is to treat these employees with the highest ethical standards and proper etiquette.

Part One

The Beginning

Protect and Maintain Your Integrity
and the Integrity of All Others

Chapter One

The Business of Conducting Business

Excellence Can Neither Justify Nor Nullify a Wrong Done

Every orchestra has a conductor whose job it is to help coordinate and guide the players of every instrument to achieve the desired result of beautiful, cohesive, and harmonious music, thus creating a soothing and peaceful sound and environment. Each member of the orchestra does his or her best to contribute to and attain this result. The musicians follow the conductor and listen closely to each other. If the conductor makes an error, knowingly or otherwise, the music will be ruined. The same applies to the musicians; all will do their utmost to avoid making mistakes. A conductor will not intentionally misguide the musicians, for this will damage his or her reputation and the reputation of the orchestra. Similarly, the orchestra's musicians will precisely follow the conductor and ensure that he or she is performing correctly, so that the orchestra's reputation, as well as their own, is protected and kept stellar.

If either the conductor or the musicians continually make errors, the orchestra will eventually lose its good musicians, its conductor, and its audience. This decline in attendance will eventually lead to the firing of either the conductor or some of the musicians or to the demise of the orchestra.

The same is true for any business entity, thus the use of the term "conducting business." The company is the orchestra, the management is the orchestra's conductor, and the employees are its musicians. All activities of a business entity must be conducted properly for employees to work cohesively and create beautiful and successful results: growth and prosperity for everyone involved. Keep in mind that to conduct business, every activity and element must be completely synchronized and readied, with every part of the organization.

The Two Internal Critical Factor Sets

Everyone in an organization must do his or her assigned tasks as well as possible and in a timely fashion for the business to succeed. Otherwise there will be chaos.

The failure or success of a business entity can be fully attributed to the way two internal critical factor sets are dealt with.

The first is the lack of ethics and of etiquette. This is much more difficult to overcome since these are related to the human component of business, the human factors, the character of the individuals that collectively make up the character of the entire company. The importance of ethics and etiquette cannot be overestimated because they will shape and affect the character of any organization, which in essence is the character of its employees, since it is the collective character of the employees that makes up the character of the business entity.

The second is incompetence and inexperience. This can be overcome with proper training, mentoring, and/or hiring experienced professionals, or even changing the company's business model.

Businesses are established with the intention to make money—and lots of it. However, to achieve this goal many steps must be taken first. It may surprise you to read that financial success does not begin with the bottom line, with dollars. It begins with finding the right people.

Typically, these are the initial activities a business entity starts with:

- A product idea.
- Choosing the right personnel to evolve the product idea.
- Selecting a strong management team.
- Setting up the right organizational structure.
- Establishing effective internal and external communication channels.
- Defining the right set of policies and procedures.

However, products, management, organizations, communication, policies, and procedures cannot survive, let alone succeed, without healthy personnel. By healthy I mean having physical, mental, and emotional health. Health in turn is the byproduct of strong ethics and proper etiquette by which every employee will conduct himself or herself and interact with others within the organization and outside of it. It is the guiding force and the guiding light for personal conduct.

The Tower of Business

Looking at Figure 1, compare a business entity to a radio or electrical tower. Now imagine that the following components of a business entity—Products, management, organization and communication—are the four legs of the tower and the policies and procedures are the concrete foundation on which each one of the tower's legs is built and supported.

No matter how strong these legs and foundation are, the tower will not withstand nature's forces such as high winds, earthquakes, or floods. Only when crossbars are installed and connected to these four legs will the tower have the strength and stability needed to survive the harsh elements. For a business entity, the crossbars are its healthy personnel. It is the healthy personnel who strengthen and support the different components that make up the business entity and enable it to succeed.

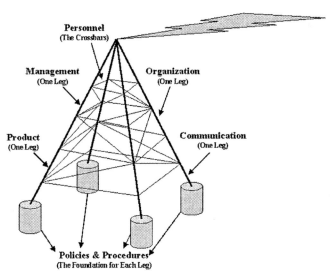

Figure 1 The tower of business

Only when the crossbars are in place will the tower be usable and productive, broadcasting television and radio programming or carrying electrical cables to transmit electricity for lighting, heating, or manufacturing. In other words, it will be delivering the products to the target markets and customers, thus generating revenue for its owners. The effect of personnel on a business is exactly that of the crossbar on the tower. The employees will carry out the company's plans to create, develop, and produce the desired products and services. However, to achieve these goals and generate the revenue stream for the business entity, all employees must be healthy mentally, emotionally, and physically. Success is so certain for this type of business entity that it could eventually become an example of how businesses must be set up and run. Its model could spread and be duplicated throughout its immediate industry and eventually to other industries and geographies. The health of the personnel would be established, as I mentioned earlier, through high ethical standards and proper etiquette within the business entity.

Going back to the example of the tower, even though the crossbars add strength to the tower, the structure must remain flexible. This flexibility is what will also help the tower survive the harsh elements. Similarly, flexibility is what every business entity needs to survive. However, there is a limit to flexibility. If the tower is too flexible, the entire structure collapses. Therefore, for flexibility to be beneficial, there must be a method for creating "structured flexibility." Structured flexibility in business is, therefore, accomplished through the freedom employees have to conduct their business and themselves within appropriate guidelines defined by the appropriate policies and procedures set forth by the business entity, which are based on strong ethics and proper etiquette.

Let me ask you this question: Which is usually left standing after strong, hurricane type winds? Is it a large old tree or a small, thin stem of grass? The answer is the small, thin stem grass! Why? Because of the stem's agility and flexibility. It sways with the wind and does not break. But the *rigid*, large old tree usually gets broken or uprooted and collapses under the force of the winds. This is exactly the same for a business entity. Flexibility must be the rule in conducting business and tending to its six components: personnel, organization, management, communication, products, and policies and procedures. However, what strengthens and controls the flexibility so that it does not create weaknesses is the ethics and etiquette by which businesses conduct themselves.

Back to Basics

With the increased demands of daily business activities, there is a very dangerous tendency to neglect the little things that make a difference and lead to success. Individuals find themselves cutting corners and eliminating steps, all in an effort to beat a deadline, finish an action item, or win a business. But in doing so, a very important aspect of conducting the business is getting ignored and, in some cases, forgotten. That aspect is "business ethics and etiquette." It is the art of "how to conduct the business." In many instances, to conduct business we must go back to basics, the basics of human and professional conduct in business.

Going back to basics means writing business plans before approving projects and products, setting up meetings with agendas, paying and compensating appropriately and not only competitively. It means valuing individuals for what they are, training and bringing up qualified candidates, showing respect, good manners, politeness, and care.

To do the right thing the right way, one needs to go back to basics. In sports, coaches say to their players when their team is falling behind in a game: "Let's go back to basics." Depending on the sport, they use comments such as "Catch the ball before you run," in football; "Keep your eye on the ball before you swing," in baseball; or "Pass the ball" in basketball. All are reminders coaches give their players when things are not going right for the entire team, not only for an individual player. The same holds true for any business entity. However, in business, basics should be followed when things are going well as well as when things are not going according to plan. Serious, honest, and fundamental questions everyone must ask when going back to basics include the following:

- Are we qualifying candidates the right way? In other words, do we understand the company's needs and match them with the right job description, experience, and qualifications?

- Are we doing the right things to motivate and retain good employees?

- Do we do enough due diligence before making decisions?

- Does every employee spend his or her time at work efficiently and productively?

- Is communication conducted effectively and efficiently, or are there too many meetings, for example, and those are not properly organized?

- Are business plans written before jumping into new businesses, new products, or new geography?

- Are employees trained properly in every aspect of the company's business and products?

- Do we have the right collateral material for internal and external use?
- Are we properly organized regarding structure and size?
- Do we have the right management structure and style for the type of business we are in?
- Are there vision and mission statements? And are they known and understood by everyone?
- Is everyone well informed about the company, products, and industry events and activities?
- Are we making the right investment in business and people?
- Are we offering our employees the right environment?

These questions as well as others must all be clearly identified, answered, internally communicated, and digested before a company can correct or improve itself, succeed, and fuel its expansion.

On the other hand, just because something is done in an ethical manner does not mean it is done right or it is the right thing for the company. For example, a company may decide to move into a new and more attractive facility even though its current location is sufficient for the time being and employees are satisfied with it. However, it may cost more in lease payments, moving expense, and disruption of work to relocate to the new facility. This obviously is not the right decision to make even though management's heart is in the right place and intentions are good. Instead the added monthly expense or moving expense could be spent directly on employees for such items as new projects, training, new equipment, bonuses, or even salary increases.

Doing the right thing in the right way covers all aspects of a business. It even gets down to such simple things as how and when to spend, how to dress, how to speak, how to conduct a meeting, how to treat others above or below you, and so on. Many of these issues will be addressed in the following chapters outlining how certain business processes and activities should be conducted—in other words, applying the right etiquette to the right activity.

The following chapters will describe and analyze how ethics and etiquette come into play and affect the six components that make up a business entity. Again, these six components of a business entity are: personnel, organization, management, communication, products, and policies and procedures. (Policies and procedures are treated as one component.)

However, before moving on to describing in more detail how ethics and etiquette are and must be intertwined with every aspect of business, I would like to present four categories, one of which every company in the world will fit into (Figure 2).

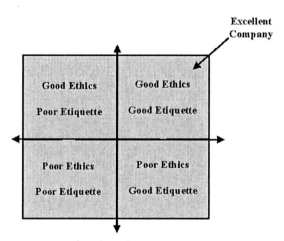

Figure 2 The four categories that describe companies

Keep in mind that a company could belong to one of the categories as a whole, but individual groups or department could fit into another.

The four simple categories that describe companies are as follows:

- Good ethics and good etiquette. These are companies that are good and know how to run their business. They are the best companies. They know the right things to do and do them right.

- Good ethics and poor etiquette. These are companies that are good but don't know how to run their business. They are companies that do the right things and want to do right by their people. However, they may fail because they are not strong in conducting their business. They need to gain experience to succeed.

- Poor ethics and good etiquette. These are companies that are bad but know how to run their business. They are bad companies in that they are not paying attention to doing the right things. However, they have good experience and the ability to run their company and conduct its business successfully. Perfect example is Enron. It takes skills and perseverance to succeed. However, these people are corrupt and unethical.

- Poor ethics and poor etiquette. These are companies that are bad overall and don't know how to run their business. They don't know how to do business; they have no experience and no ability. These companies come up and go down in the blink of an eye.

We have all known of, or worked for, companies that fall into one of these categories. If we have worked for them, we have experienced either the trials and tribulations or the triumphs and successes. None of the companies that fall into one of these categories are guaranteed to remain there. Good companies can go bad and bad companies can become good, just as weak companies can become strong and succeed and successful companies can become weak and disappear. The recipe for companies who want to attain and maintain their high status and position is to blend high ethics and proper etiquette. The following chapters will present and describe the ingredients of this recipe.

Chapter Two

Eye-Opening Experiences:
What I Learned and How I Learned It

The First Company I Worked For

The first company I worked for was a developer of Point Of Sale (POS) terminals and inventory control systems for the automotive industry. I will refer to it as the POS Company. I was hired as an Associate Digital Logic Design Engineer. I had one semester left before graduating from San Jose State University when I was hired. I was proud and full of excitement because I was hired before getting my undergraduate degree and was earning a very good annual salary. I thought they must think highly of my potential to become a great digital logic design engineer and contribute to the company and, in time, to the whole industry. Full of excitement, I used to get to work around 7:30 AM and get right to work. I had a lot to learn. I also wanted to live up to the trust that management put in me by hiring me and giving me the opportunity to grow and prosper.

Finally my first assignment arrived. I couldn't wait to get started. I went to work the next day and began researching and reading up on topics relevant to the design. One week later I was ready to begin schematic drawings. One day, when I got to my office in the morning, halfway through my design efforts, I got a completed set of schematics for the project I was working on dropped on my desk, before the project's due date. I looked at the name on the drawings to see who did the work. The name was that of my manager. He stopped by my cubicle just about the time I was ready to go to his. He explained that he wanted to help me learn and understand by seeing how things are done, how schematics were drawn and created, and so forth. I was totally fine with this and began to study the new schematics, learning new things, confirming some of my design as being correct, and began building the test board in compliance with my manager's design schematics. The board was completed, tested, and released on time with documentation. My task was done. Now the waiting began for a new project.

The second project came along and my excitement came back with it. Again, I began my preparation for the design. But the same thing happened again. My manager delivered the completed schematics to my cubicle, again before the project's due date. This time he told me to build the test board. I was beginning to get suspicious and discouraged. However, the project was done again, completed, and verified on time.

The third project came along. This time I worked as fast as I could to get it done before my manager delivered a completed set of schematics to me. Again he beat me to it.

This was where I drew the line. I called him to a meeting room and expressed my concerns and disappointment in his actions, his management style, and the fact that I was not being given the full time allotted for completing the projects and doing my job, the job I was hired to do. I told him I was not learning anything since he was doing it all for me. I needed mentoring and training, not spoon-feeding and pampering. He promised to pay attention to my needs and said that he would not do the work again. I thought this was great. I was able to talk to my manager and voice my concerns without getting chewed out.

As the company grew, the number of projects increased, which meant more personnel in the group and a new organizational structure. With the new organization, I got a new manager who reported to my previous manager. My first manager was promoted. I did not get to find out if my first manager meant what he promised. I was somewhat disappointed and concerned with the possibility of losing the agreement I had made with him about allowing me to do my projects. By that time I had gotten my BSEE and had learned quite a bit more about digital logic design through personal efforts and help from experienced colleagues. Even though there were no new projects assigned to me, I was having a lot of fun learning from other engineers.

One of the features of the company's primary products was identified as having problems relative to competitors' solutions. It was the quality of the displays of the Point-of-Sales terminals. I took an interest in this. I took the challenge upon myself to find a solution to the problem. I worked during my off hours and lunch time to find the solution. And I did it! I was filled with excitement and could hardly wait to share my findings with my new manager and the rest of the team. So I wrote the description of the problem and the way to solve it. I drew the schematics and modified one of the terminals to demonstrate the improvement achieved to the rest of the team and to management, including my new boss. Management as a whole had to be involved because the display was part of every product the company made. The management team was very pleased with the improvement to the display quality and was impressed with my initiative to fix the problem. However, to my surprise, my new boss began to interrogate me and ask how I found the solution, apparently trying to find out whether I knew what I was doing or was just having good luck. He then began to try to find weaknesses and flaws in my solution and recommended to management that they not approve the modification to the displays until further evaluation was completed. This project was put on the back burner and eventually covered up by other projects.

A few months following those events, I submitted my resignation. Less than a year after that, the company's business deteriorated to the point where a major layoff took place. Two of the people laid off were my managers. The reason for the company's business deterioration was better display-quality products from competitors, which chipped away at their customer base. However, I believe that the main reason for the company's weakness was that too many talented employees left the company, delaying introduction of its new products, thus further weakening the company's competitiveness.

I truly did not want to leave the POS Company because I liked the company's products; I liked the people in my group and in other groups, including members of the senior management. The company's facilities were great, new, and clean and the location was very convenient. I was also learning a lot about design processes and the market segment we were focused on. Despite all these benefits, I knew it was time to leave.

The Second Company I Worked For

Following the POS Company job, in the summer of 1984, I went to work for a government contractor who developed flight simulators for NATO. I will call this company the Government Contractor. I was now a staff engineer with secret clearance, hired to design flight simulator interface cards. These cards enabled advanced computers to simulate fighter jet cockpit experiences used in new pilot training programs. When I joined the company, my project was waiting for me. I was nervous, wondering if my new manager would be like my first manager at the POS Company and want to do the design himself. After a few weeks of training and acquiring the necessary knowledge about the products in general and how things are done in a government-related business, the design began.

Every morning I used to go to work anxious and concerned that the project schematics would be on my desk, completed by my boss. As the weeks went by, I calmed down and lost my anxiety completely and was able to fully concentrate on my project's design. The design was fully completed, the test board built and tested verifying the functionality of the design, and the documentation written and delivered, *ahead of schedule*. I did it. I was on top of the world again.

I was relieved that none of the experiences I went through at the POS Company occurred here. My respect for my manager grew stronger as time went by. The group I belonged to was developing the complete flight simulator. My completed interface cards were only a portion of the entire product. Other members of the group were still working to complete their portion of the overall system design. For the next few months I worked with other members of the group helping with their projects since I did not have another project to work on. I basically considered myself as an available resource for whoever needed support, a team effort. Little did I know that this would come back to haunt me personally later on.

Annual performance reviews were to be conducted during my idle time, that is, during the time when I did not have a project to work on but was still busy helping the rest of the team to complete the entire project. New project assignments were the responsibility of managers, my manager in my case. I was pumped up and ready to get a big pat on the back for a job well done, a good raise, and possibly a promotion, not a new title but to the next grade level. Was I wrong! Because I had completed my project months ahead of schedule and had appeared idle because no new projects were assigned to me, or to the rest of the group for that matter, my manager gave me a less than average performance evaluation. I was shocked and immensely disappointed. When I mentioned to him that it was his responsibility to assign projects to his subordinates and not my fault for not having a new project to work on after my first project was completed and delivered fully functional and ahead of schedule, my manager replied, "I understand and agree that you did a very good job, Vahé. But I cannot take the blame for not assigning a new project to you even though it was my responsibility to do so." I was speechless. I had to give it to him, though; at least he was honest.

A few months later, after I had been with the company for almost two years, layoffs hit again. This was when I decided to get my MBA and move out of engineering and into marketing, into the business side of the high-tech industry, hoping the grass would be greener on the other side. I forgot that, as the Irish say, "there are forty shades of green" and I had experienced only a few of the shades, not knowing that there were lighter and darker shades yet to be uncovered.

What I Learned

"So what did all this mean? What did I just go through?" were questions I continually asked myself after leaving the first two companies I worked for. I did not get the answers until I had enough experience under my belt, until I had grown personally and professionally in matters of character. Only then did I understand and appreciate the effects of the human factor in business and on business.

The problems I experienced are neither rare nor specific to the high-tech industry. They happen in all industries and at all levels of any organization.

Again, the common denominator is the human factor. Businesses and their organizations are managed and run by people. Each organization has its own identity and culture, created and influenced by its personnel—individuals who have their own identities and characteristics, which will collectively make up the corporate culture. The values and principles by which these individuals live and conduct their personal lives will become the values and principles of the company, and will determine how it conducts itself. They will affect the policies and procedures by which the corporation conducts its business, treats its employees and constituencies, and nurtures its managers.

Consider my first set of professional experiences with my first two managers at the POS Company. What my first manager appeared to be doing was the right thing: mentoring and training the inexperienced employee (myself, in this case) and teaching the design processes, methodology, and systems. The professional training process is basically an upbringing, just as with a newborn child. One must protect, teach, nurture (mentally, physically, emotionally, spiritually), and guide the child through the various stages of growing up, from infant to toddler to adolescent to teenager until young adulthood and sometimes beyond. Depending on the individual, sometimes more handholding is needed and sometimes less. Sometimes handholding is needed in certain situations and not in others. In any event, the process must be completed. However, the time comes when this handholding must cease. Otherwise, the child will never grow up to become independent and develop his or her own personality and character as an individual. He or she will never be able to make decisions or take actions without supervision and intervention by an authority figure: a teacher, a parent, or in the case of business, a manager. Therefore, there is a proper etiquette to handle certain situations. When this etiquette is not followed, the damage to the employee, the group, even the company as a whole, is irreparable.

The actions of my first manager showed that either he did not have enough knowledge of proper etiquette to train an amateur design engineer or he did not choose to use it. Instead, he took the easier and quicker way to get the job done, which was to complete the schematics without giving me a chance to do the work myself and learn from my mistakes, asking questions and researching new ideas as I went along. Such actions by managers impact not only themselves but also their employees.

The effects of the managers' poor etiquette include the following:

- Adversely affecting the new employee's learning process.
- Damaging the new employee's self-esteem and confidence.
- Missing the opportunity to hear a new idea or to improve an existing process or method.

- Damaging the reputation of the new employee among his or her peers and the rest of the company. Colleagues would think this employee is the manager's puppet.

- Taking time away from his or her other duties, such as managing everyone else in their group and all of the group's activities, thus impacting other parts of the organization and in turn the company's business and performance.

- Paying an employee without sufficient return, i.e., minimizing the company's return on its investment in this new employee, especially when the employee is being trained.

- Weakening that area of the organization where the untrained employee works. This is worse than having a vacant position. It will have an adverse impact on the individual's career and eventually on the industry as a whole if more managers follow this style of management. This is basically creating a wasted resource.

- Taking away from the manager's own personal time by performing the duties of another person. Not only will the manager not have enough time during work to get the job done, but it will also take away from his time after work. This could have been time with family, friends, professional associations, self-improvement, or simple rest and relaxation.

- Causing the company to lose good young employees who could have developed into stars.

- Causing the company to lose revenue and its reputation.

Now let's go back to the incidents with my second manager at the POS Company. Here, my manager's ego was at play in a big way. The thought that an amateur designer could come up with the solution without his help must have injured his ego. For him, it was better to discredit the results and the employee rather than let go of the ego, understand the solution, and jointly work to firm up the solution for the betterment of the entire company. But by discrediting the employee and/or the solution, not only did the company pass up an opportunity to correct a product weakness and help its business potential, but also it weakened an employee's morale, an employee who was sincere in his efforts to help everyone—the company, the team, and himself—by taking the initiative to make a positive contribution to the company's products and competitiveness.

The second manager's actions not only lacked the proper etiquette; they also were unethical because they attacked my credibility and reputation. This was demoralizing to me and to everyone in the organization who had a sense of what was taking place. This action became even more damaging to the entire operation since the manager did accomplish what he set out to do, and that was to successfully derail the efforts to implement a solution to the company's product flaw. Actions such as these can have long-lasting and adverse effects on any company, its business and employees. The effects of unethical actions on the part of managers may include the following:

- Demoralizing the individual in question and the entire organization.

- Causing employees to freeze and not take any initiative, to be unable to think for themselves and make decisions without wasting time waiting for approvals. It is important to take direction and get approval before moving forward on certain activities; however, direction must be set at the outset for all employees to know where they are heading, when, and how.

- Creating resentments and possible rebellion against the manager. This will create tremendous difficulties for the manager involved and for the rest of the company's management.

- Creating a "yes" culture, which becomes a time sink for management and causes revenue and opportunity loss for the company; it also derails creativity, causing the company to become stale and stagnant.

- Causing distrust of all levels of management by the individual contributor employees.

- Losing good employees.

In summary, not only did I need to get the proper training in digital logic design, but also my managers needed just as much training in management. Specifically, they needed to know how to mentor, motivate, support, and protect members of their team as well as individual contributors in other parts of the organization.

In the case of my manager at the Government Contractor, his actions were completely unethical. He covered up his mistakes and blamed me by misrepresenting my achievements and misleading management by providing false information to protect himself. The actions of managers who do such things have far-reaching effects on the individual, the entire company, and the industry. The process of conducting performance reviews for employees involves management presenting a justification for why a particular employee should receive a specific increase or decrease in compensation, title, position, and responsibility. This justification should be qualified by many factors, including achievements, attendance, behavior, and the total progress of the employee in question. To receive a less than average review means that the employee's manager presented information to senior management indicating that the employee did not do a good job. When the information used in the justification is untrue, then the manager has not exercised fairness and honesty; he was unethical. Basically, company management was given inaccurate information about the particular employee. In other words, they were misled and lied to. When this type of management style prevails in the industry, the industry as a whole will suffer. It leads to the attitude of "everyone for him or herself" instead of a teamwork mentality. This style of management and treatment of employees has very adverse effects on the entire business entity. The following are more effects of managers' unethical actions in addition to those previously mentioned:

- Damaging the employee's reputation.
- Damaging the employee's motivation, commitment, and achievements.
- Decreasing the employee's wages.
- Laying off the employee due to an incorrect perception of his or her performance and contributions as being nonproductive or weak.
- Promoting unfairness and deceit.
- Creating an atmosphere in which the employee focuses on protecting himself or herself rather than on doing what is right.
- Losing a sense of teamwork.
- Creating doubts about the employee's original hiring manager's judgment and ability to choose the right personnel for the position and the company. Actions such as these will have far-reaching effects on the company and its employees at all levels.

- Losing good employees.
- Causing damage to the company's reputation and ability to generate revenue.

Keep in mind that the effects of positive or negative actions will not be contained within the boundaries of a company's buildings or campus. They will spill over to other companies and entire industries. Employees and managers move from one company to another and their experiences will shape their future decisions, behavior, and attitude, which could either lead to productive or destructive results. This is one of the major reasons that actions must be well thought out before they are taken, especially by management personnel.

Similar to many professionals in all types of industries, I do not exclude myself from having made mistakes. I have made many. Some unethical and some showing poor etiquette. However, I believe the key is to recognize, acknowledge, and accept the mistakes made and work to correct them and not repeat them ever again.

The Wisdom in What I Learned

Don't Do Someone Else's Work Without His or Her Consent or Knowledge

Question to Understand, Not to Discredit

Do Not Hide Behind Your Employees

Do Not Allow Events or People to Rob You of Your Confidence, Drive, Commitment or Integrity

Gain Respect by Acknowledging Your Mistakes and Weaknesses As Well As Your Strengths

Flexibility Comes From Confidence

Protect and Maintain Your Integrity and the Integrity of All Others

Excellence Can Neither Justify Nor Nullify a Wrong Done

Part Two

Business Ethics and Etiquette

Business Ethics
Is Doing the Right Thing;
Business Etiquette
Is Doing the Right Thing
The Right Way

Chapter Three

Personnel

Excellence Will Neither Justify Nor Nullify Misbehavior

When I had been a marketing manager at Company SC for two weeks, my manager resigned. I was idle for a few weeks after that but was educating myself on the company's products and business in general. Finally, the acting manager came to me one morning and dropped a bound document on my desk. He said, "This information is about the company's efforts to penetrate this new market. It has been tried twice before without success. Do you want to give it a try?" I jumped to the opportunity and accepted the task. To make a long story short, with a strong and synergistic team effort, eighteen months later we had defined a new product and won the largest customer in that market, kicking the competition out. At a project review meeting where we discussed the custom product we were developing for this large customer, I was present and ready to support the group director in his presentation. I was also excited about the possibility of getting recognition for my efforts. Instead, when my manager presented the project and the efforts leading to its success, he took the credit for orchestrating the entire strategy to penetrate and win the customer. Even though the head of the product division corrected this later on, the damage was already done.

Everything starts with people. The greatest institution in the world was founded on this premise. The government and country of the United States of America was founded "for the people, by the people." People run the government. If they are ethical and honest, then the country is destined for greatness.

It is ironic, though, that so many leaders of countries and companies, managers and executives, agree with this concept but fail to act accordingly. Managers and CEOs use the phrase "our people are our most important assets'"; however, their organizations and companies continue to pay little attention to their employees, their needs, and their well-being. These needs are all-encompassing and must be satisfied in a balanced way to include their surroundings and environment, and their physical, mental, and emotional needs. The needs of all the employees must be taken into consideration. Take, for example, the need for handicapped access; this access accommodates a very small minority, but still it is considered important and is provided.

The foundation for any company is the employee. That is where the growth begins and where it also ends. It begins with a number of employees gathered to create a team. Multiple teams create a group. Multiple groups create a department. Multiple departments make up a division or a business unit, multiple divisions or business units create a company, and so on. Organizational structure will differ from one business entity to the other based on the business type, objectives, and requirements. However, to create a successful organization, positive human factors and strong personnel must be present.

So much of a company's success rests on its personnel that it should come as no surprise that those companies who attract and retain good employees by taking care of them survive all the trials and tribulations of their industry as well as difficult economic times much better and for much longer than other companies in the same industry that don't have and follow the same mentality about the importance of taking care of their own employees. The successful companies become leaders of their industries and influencers of companies in other industries over time. In reality successful companies do not force their employees to stay on board and contribute; it is the employees themselves who decide to stay without any coercion, bribery, or arm-twisting. For such companies, employees will have the desire and determination to contribute and produce at the highest levels. They will be committed to achieving any goal and objective the company may have or put forth to them. It is this determination and attitude expressed by the employees that propels these companies to leadership status. It becomes a matter of the employees having pride in themselves, their organization, and the people who lead them. This is when a gem, a diamond, of an organization is created, beautiful yet strong, clear and bright even when the external environment, the economy or the specific industry, maybe dark and cloudy.

In many instances, individuals at all levels of an organization are quick to judge others at any level of the organization for something they have done or said before making an effort in trying to understand the reasons and motives for the particular behavior displayed by those individuals. The behavior that attracted the judgment could be the individual's performance, treatment of and interaction with others, the individual's opinions and views, or just his or her disposition. Good or bad, sometimes people render an opinion without even having all the facts. This is especially prevalent in cases where excess or unbalanced attention and care is given to the management of the company and the privileged few as compared to the rest of the company. This habit causes opinions to be formulated and judgments passed by lower-level personnel driven by the feeling of double standards or unfairness, preferential treatment, or neglect among employees.

Companies spend enormous amounts of time and money on the nonhuman aspects of their businesses, especially at the higher levels of the organization, which further drives a wedge between these different levels. Such expenditure on nonhuman items includes the following:

- Elaborate buildings and offices.
- Expensive furniture.
- Cars and other personal perks such as mansions, expensive memberships, and boats.
- Company jets.
- Unnecessary expenditure on business activities, especially during insufficient budget allocation or even budget cuts.
- Excessively high salaries, bonuses, raises, and other elements to the compensation packages of management.

All of the above is basically done at the expense of employees' well-being. It's surprising to hear managers of companies that do offer elaborate packages to the privileged few while ignoring the needs of the rest of the employees make comments to the effect that they don't know or understand why their company is having negative experiences. Some of the negative results and experiences managers question include the following:

- Their business is down.
- The company's productivity is down.
- Employees are unhappy and there is a general deterioration of the work environment.
- There is too much attrition.
- They cannot attract and hire good new employees.

This type of behavior and questioning or comments by managers is clear proof that they are not in touch with their employees.

Personnel Ethics

Emotions Come from Being Human and Caring:
They Are Destructive When Born Out of Insecurity

Employees at all levels of the organization recognize unfairness and double standards because such actions do take place in personal life as well. Those who experience such treatment will have negative feelings about the company and its management.

A perfect example of employees reacting negatively is when revenues and profits for the business entity are going down, but certain employees are still being paid enormous salaries or receiving perks not available to others. Outrageous bonuses are being paid out to CEOs and vice presidents while benefits, salaries, even jobs are being eliminated from the rest of the company. Feelings of being used and abused set in. In addition, employees will rightfully interpret the messages communicated by these actions as being "everyone for him- or herself." Employees then are likely to develop and experience more negative feelings including the following:

- Desire to disobey.
- Lack of motivation.
- Lack of commitment.
- Distrust.
- Unwillingness to sacrifice.
- Neglected, unimportant, belittled, or betrayed.

Not surprisingly, the results of such feelings are also negative for the company. The outcome of employees' negative feelings include the following:

- Resignations and attrition.
- Decline in productivity.
- Deterioration of the work environment.

While the employees demonstrate these negative behaviors, most of the time subconsciously, the company will develop an unwanted reputation of being an uncaring and unfair organization filled with self-serving, self-centered management driven by greed. Employees will then begin serving their own needs by becoming self-serving and self-centered themselves or search for and depart to a more favorable company. The negative effects of attrition will not only impact organizations and individual groups within companies, but also they will harm the companies themselves.

As personnel move to other organizations or companies, work disruption takes place affecting the operations of the group that experiences the attrition. Taking on a new employee means that there has to be training, which means time and money spent. When this training is unnecessary, the time and money are being wasted and could have been spent differently. This will eventually lead to questions about the soundness and health of that particular group, its management, and its work environment, which may be causing the attrition to begin with.

If one or two employees do this or a very small percentage of employees express concern and the percentage remains constant for a long time, then it may be safe to assume it is the employees and not the environment or management. Still, attention must be given to this to monitor, confirm, and validate. However, when the company's doors become "revolving doors" where employees come and go very quickly, only staying for a short period of time, less than twelve to eighteen months, then it is safe to assume that there is a problem within the company and it needs to be fixed quickly.

Problems such as these occur in companies of all sizes and types and in all industries. Large publicly traded companies have them, as do startup companies, companies with 100 employees, and those with 10,000 employees. High-tech as well as low-tech, automotive, medical, and financial industries all go through it.

When companies are first established, issues such as these usually do not exist. The reason is that the founders of the business entity are busy creating the product and the company, laying the foundation for their business model. In addition, the originators of the product idea will usually choose those individuals with whom they have most in common or whom they know very well and have possibly worked with in the past. As these startups begin to grow in size and number of employees, so will the potential for the issues listed above to begin surfacing. It is, therefore, crucial to the success and long-term survival of the company to carefully and closely monitor such behaviors so that necessary corrective actions can be taken at the first signs of such problems.

All startup companies are created with the right group of people getting together in an effort to bring a product idea to fruition. The first task for the individual, or individuals, with the product idea is to recruit the right team to further develop the product idea, ensuring along the way that the personalities and characteristics of the different individuals match and complement one another.

One of the most important realizations for any business entity is to recognize which skills are missing and which are present. These include functional skills, such as engineering, marketing, and sales, and interpersonal skills needed to build the organization and its business. If one could do everything individually, then there would have been many more single-person organizations in the high-tech industry, or in any other industry for that matter, lots of one-man shows. However, this is not the case nor will it ever be.

Negative Human Factors

Ethical People Respect and Promote Equality

Whenever a group of people get together to create an organization, the human factors come into play. The good health of these human factors must be taken very seriously, protected and nurtured if success is sought. Numerous elements, negative and positive, make up the entire set of human factors. However, I will discuss only those that, I believe, have the strongest and most serious adverse impact and effect on the business entity. I will refer to these factors as the *Negative Human Factors (NHF)* and they are as follows:

I.   Destructive competitiveness.

II.   Disagreements, arguments, and frustration.

III. Destructive criticism.

IV.   Anger, sensitivity, emotional ups and downs and personality conflicts.

V.   Immaturity.

VI.   Greed, jealousy, and blame.

VII. Impatience.

VIII. Misuse of rank and seniority.

IX.   Prejudice and ignorance relative to gender, age, and culture.

X.   Dishonesty, lying, deceit, and manipulation.

As I stated earlier, there are many other NHFs that will have an adverse impact on the health of a business including hatred, holding grudges, complaining, and many others. However, the impact of the latter items is not as far-reaching and destructive as the ten NHFs I have chosen.

The presence of any of the ten NHFs will have an adverse effect on the business entity and its survival. If not managed and channeled properly toward resolution, these NHFs will grow and become infectious. For human factors to be productive and have a positive effect on an organization, the highest standard of ethics and the most proper etiquette must be practiced. Otherwise, there can be no success under any circumstances. It does not matter how powerful and experienced the employees or management are, it does not matter how well organized the company is, or how superior its products are—the outcome in the long run will most certainly be the failure of the business. When these NHFs take hold in an organization, the reversal of their effects is usually very difficult to achieve. Figure 3 demonstrates the relationship between NHFs, the company health, and chances for failure. As NHFs increase inside a company, so will the company's chances for failure. The shaded area in Figure 3 labeled as "1" demonstrate the presence of very small amounts of NHFs in the company. This is usually true for very small companies, in their startup phase. It is not possible to have zero negative human factors in any company . Therefore, the health of the company is good while very few NHFs are present. As the company grows and hires more employees, there will be an increase in NHFs, as shown in Figure 3. The presence of any one, a combination of, or all of these factors with different intensity will increase the company's chances for failure. The shaded area labeled "2" describes a large company that has significant amounts of negative, uncontrolled NHFs. However, some companies will survive the presence of these NHFs and continue to exist because over time they have put in place mechanisms that deal with such personnel issues and, in addition, they have the necessary resources to manage them. Such companies are usually old, very large in size and revenue, with a long history and track record, but not necessarily very profitable. Figure 3 shows that such companies are unhealthy and the chance of failure is always high and present.

In the remainder of this chapter I will discuss in more detail the symptoms and effects of NHFs on any business and its personnel. Keep in mind that this is not meant to be a course in psychology; it is a common-sense analysis based on personal and professional experience of some of the most damaging behaviors and characteristics of people in the workplace.

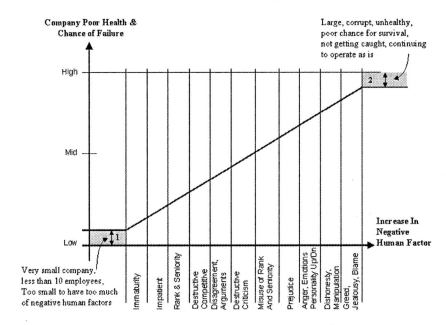

Figure 3 Impact of NHFs on a business entity

NHF-I: Destructive Competitiveness

Without competition there can be no advancements of any kind. Competitiveness is a wonderful attribute to have if used ethically and at appropriate times, with the proper etiquette. After all, many economies, including the U.S. economy, are based on competition: and their health is dependent on the health of the competitors and their ability to compete. Taking this further, if one thinks about it, what enables competition and participation in competitive activities is, after all, people. It is people who compete and the ethics of the competition is dependent upon these people's ethical standards. In business, competition is divided into external and internal competition.

External competition occurs when companies compete to win customer business in an effort to increase revenue and gain market share. (Even though external competition involves people, competitive strategies and tactics are not within the scope of this book. External competition at the human factor level will be addressed later on in this section.)

Internal competition, on the other hand, focuses on the competitiveness of individuals within the same company or organization. It is the treatment of colleagues—of each other—while competing that must be of utmost importance for businesses to identify and understand. Individual characteristics that could cause problems for a company will be unearthed if the activity is not conducted with the highest of ethics.

I define internal competitiveness as "the efforts of one or more individuals to gain the acceptance and approval of one or more other individuals." The acceptance and approval can be for an idea, opinion, plan, or decision of an individual or of individuals in general, including of themselves. This acceptance and approval is sought from any level of the organization. It is dangerous, however, when competitiveness for winning approval becomes an obsession, because this is when disregard of ethics and integrity can occur and self-serving behavior takes over.

If competitiveness is exercised to self-serve or to discredit another employee, it will have widespread and far-reaching negative effects on the entire organization. It is a behavior that will cause a chain reaction where individual competition leads to group competition, and group competition leads to a disjointed organization, eventually leading to the fracture and collapse of the company.

It is perfectly appropriate for any employee to try to do the best work possible to get ahead, to receive a promotion, or to get approval for a budget or whatever the goal of the position or task at hand is. This means doing better work than a colleague, a co-worker. If it is done with the intention of one doing his or her best with the benefit of the organization and business in mind, then this type of interaction is healthy for an organization and promotes excellence and leadership. This can be like magic that will touch every area of the business. It will instill an attitude of openness and cooperation toward a common goal.

The thing to keep in mind when competing, however, is to always address the issues at hand and not the person or persons when discussing an issue or having a disagreement. When competitiveness is always conducted ethically and with the proper etiquette without insults or put-down of others, people will be more open and receptive to new ideas presented by the other side. Why? Because of the absence of hidden agendas. Having a hidden agenda is one of the causes of unhealthy, destructive competition within an organization. When colleagues operate with hidden agendas, it signifies lack of confidence, insecurity, distrust, and unethical plans on the part of the individual or individuals having the hidden agenda. This will lead to unfair competitiveness and foul play. Whether it continues undetected or not, the effects of operating with hidden agendas are very damaging to the organization. When these agendas are uncovered, the damage and ill effects of such behavior will be temporary, lasting until those individuals are reprimanded and their actions corrected or reversed. On the other hand, when a hidden agenda is not detected, the negative effects are very serious. The negative effects of hidden agendas include the following:

- Presenting the wrong image of individuals or other groups.
- Misleading the organization and causing it to veer off course.
- Hampering the growth of other businesses causing significant opportunity losses for the company.
- Misrepresenting the company to the outside world, putting forth the wrong image and reputation.

Acting in a competitive manner is like walking a tightrope. It could be viewed favorably at times, while other times it is misinterpreted and viewed as a way for the individual or individuals to show off, undermine, bring down, attack, or step on others. This is one of the reasons why so many individuals don't take the initiative or voice their opinions about various matters critical to the success of the company, for fear of being erroneously labeled or characterized as being a show off, or attacking others. It is therefore critical for management to promote, but also closely monitor, competitiveness within groups and among employees and identify the fine line and encourage participation.

Working for Company SJ as vice president of marketing, I raised the issue of product development delays and how these delays were adversely affecting our chances to win more customers and expand our business and market share. My intentions were not to get anyone in trouble; I wanted to raise the bar and get the engineering department to deliver on its commitments and not continuously reschedule the product delivery dates. The CEO of the company misinterpreted my actions, labeling them as a finger-pointing exercise as well as labeling me as a non-team player. Needless to say, the products never came out and the company suffered losing most of its customer base and shrinking from approximately ninety employees to under thirty in less than nine months.

Competition is a driving force used to achieve and reach a goal or milestone. However, to achieve the goal or reach the milestone, competition must be healthy. Healthy competition is the result of pride, self-confidence, and self-respect. It does not mean one can look down on others, step on them, or discredit them to achieve the goal. In this process, the competitor must pull in others, the rest of the organization, to outdo an individual effort. All this must be done with good intentions, however, not out of mischief. Ethical competition and competition with proper etiquette ensure that everyone can be certain that the information presented is true and the individual's motives respectful. Both the self and the opposition are respected in the process. Let's consider the following example.

When two individuals, colleagues, who work for the same company, are competing for funds to finance their projects, they must present information that is correct, accurate and truthful to the decision makers. In addition, *all* the information must be presented; nothing should be held back or hidden to skew the views and opinions of the decision makers. It is unethical to knowingly present incorrect and incomplete information or to cover up information from the decision makers. The result of such action will most likely lead to a wrong decision or to an untimely one, leading in turn to a wrong or untimely action being taken. In either case, the organization as a whole will suffer the consequences. Eventually the truth will surface and the reputation of the individual will be damaged, permanently. Sharing all and accurate information is vital to any organization and to any decision since it facilitates the verification efforts of the information presented through discussion and dialogue. When the information is validated, it will strengthen and support the position of the individual presenting that information. It is also important for future requests made by the same individual for his or her current actions to be ethical. This type of behavior will serve as a trust builder and facilitate the effectiveness and success of future activities and interaction.

Sharing the correct and complete set of information with the right people at the right time is not only necessary and a must for internal activities, but also for external activities, as in the case of two companies competing for a particular customer or business. Truthful and correct information must be presented to the customer because once the customer determines that the information was misleading or incomplete, the business and the relationship will be lost for a very long time if not forever.

My view is that "it is better to lose the business than to lose the relationship with a customer." A business can always be won at a later time, but relationships may never be reestablished once severed. The other effect of misinforming a target customer to win the business is that the customer will make decisions with an incorrect set of information, which could eventually lead to business loses. With loss of business, the survival of the customer's company and its employees will be at risk as well, and this takes us back to the title of this book, *Business Is The People.*

Individuals or organizations must use common sense when determining the timing and amount of information they should communicate to their customers. The key factor to consider during this process is to ensure that the customer will not be adversely affected by the decision of not communicating certain information at a certain time. If one knows, for example, that the customer is planning to start production in thirty days but the product will not be ready for three months, the decision and steps that need to be taken are clear. Tell the truth. Be ethical. Protect the customer. Retain the customer's trust and respect for the long-term health of the relationship and future business.

As vice president of marketing and sales for Company OK, my organization was responsible for all products and customer activities. The company's latest product came out of production with major flaws. It was determined that to correct these flaws and meet the intended specifications of the device would take a minimum of three months. That was also how long it would take before customers could receive and use this product. However, I was asked not to share the correct date with customers if they asked. One of our key customers was planning their production run using this device in a product they were to introduce that would be an industry first, a major product for the company. Having found out about the problems and delays with our product, I decided to join my marketing manager at a meeting with the customer to give an update of our product's status and share this new information, and work out a recovery plan. During the meeting with this customer, the customer's project manager asked for the latest and exact delivery date for the device. I gave him the true date, "three months from now." This would completely kill any hopes for revenue from this product for this manager. With this information, he asked my opinion for what actions I would recommend for them to take. I knew their delay threshold was thirty days. The choice was clear and it was to wait for our device to arrive three months from now and hope that it will work as planned, by then. I told him to halt production. If I had not done that, the customer would have lost millions of dollars. Their product would have been manufactured to the point where they would need our device and then they would have had to wait for at least three months. The market window would have closed and their reputation would have been damaged. In addition, the project manager would have lost his credibility and possibly his job. On the other hand, the reputation of the company I worked for would have been tarnished and so would mine as an industry professional.

All these factors must be kept in mind in situations like this, and the fact that whatever industry one works in is a very small industry. One never knows when one could run into someone he or she worked with, worked for, or supported in the past. If the relationship with these individuals were not healthy, one would be jeopardizing his or her future because no one will want to deal with such an individual due to bad experiences in the past.

The relationship with this customer was kept intact. However, my relationship with my boss was damaged to the point where I left the company one month following those events.

NHF-II: Disagreements, Arguments, and Frustration

Disagreements are vital to any business as long as they take place with the proper ethics, intention and etiquette. I call these disagreements "professional disagreements."

Even when they are heated and result in arguments, they are good as long as they are kept professional and not personal. Disagreements and arguments can be labeled "professional" when the attack is directed at the issues being argued rather than the individuals arguing them. These disagreements and arguments can generate tremendous brainpower, creativity, inventiveness, and even unity. How? Simple. In an ideal world, when there is a disagreement, the parties involved must perform more research to defend and back up their positions. In doing so, if the conduct is ethical, the correct or better solution or answer may be determined and verified while new things are learned along the way. This will result in the differing parties coming to terms and working on the common solution with complete commitment.

When two or more individuals have differing views or opinions about a specific issue, a disagreement is born. The differing opinion could be about a strategy to win a customer, a way to organize a team, or whether to include certain information in the user's manual or not. This occurs in every facet of one's life, personal as well as professional. The proper etiquette, though, is to establish a dialogue and a channel of communication to discuss the matter like mature and professional adults. It is only through the exchange of varying views and opinions— through dialogue—that there can be openness to new things. This dialogue is what creates unity and establishes respect and maturity throughout the organization. In other words, the energy that the disagreements generate must be channeled properly to create a positive outcome; otherwise, chaos will exist.

If the matter is left to fester, arguments will replace dialogue and discussion, eventually leading to frustration and the fracture of the organization. Instead of unity, various individuals, groups, or departments will feel isolated from the rest of the organization, resulting in a disjointed operation that will eventually cease to function. Isolating a piece of an organization basically renders that piece useless.

One of two things can be the cause of frustration:

- The individual's incompatibility with his or her role or position due to inability, inexperience, or the lack of clear direction.

- The individual's incompatibility with the organization.

In the case of the individual's inability, inexperience, and incompatibility with his or her role or position, it is up to the individual and management to raise the issue and review the skills and capabilities of the employee in question and determine the best course of action for the individual and the company to take. The individual must first perform a careful and honest self-evaluation. If there are ways to acquire the knowledge through training or self-education, then they should be used. Otherwise it is in the best interest of the employee and the company for the employee to be reassigned to a new position or role. This initiative demonstrated by the employee will actually be perceived positively. When an employee recognizes his or her weakness and tries to improve it, shows that he or she has these traits:

- Concern for the business and others.
- Self-confidence.
- The desire to learn and improve.
- The desire to have the opportunity to contribute by acquiring tasks that are in line with his or her capabilities and position.

This is very important for the employee and the company since it is an issue of performance and getting the job done. If the cause of frustration is an organizational issue, management needs to hear the individual's concerns, then research and analyze the matter. Remember, if the organization is broken, the employees will not be able to perform their tasks and meet the company's requirements and expectations. It could be a policy, a procedure, or the organizational structure that is the culprit here and not the individual employee. However, it could also be people-related. Organizational issues causing frustration for employees include the following:

- Restrictive organizational structure and processes where the employees have to get permission for every activity. They are neither encouraged nor allowed to make the smallest of decisions on their own without management's intervention. In such a case it is easier and cheaper to hire junior employees and tell them what to do. Even though comments and statements are made to the effect that employees at all levels are empowered and encouraged to make decision, in reality actions don't match what is being conveyed verbally. One point must be kept in mind at all times when dealing with this issue: if management does not trust their employees to make wise decisions, then those employees should not have been hired or retained in the first place. There has to be trust up and down the organization. Managers cannot make all the decisions all the time. Managers must learn to delegate and mentor in order to develop all areas of the organization.

- Rigid organizational structure. Rigidity is also part of being restrictive; however, here it refers to being close-minded, unwilling to change anything—not a structure, not a policy, not a process, not a strategy. As in restrictive organizations, managers might as well hire junior personnel and just tell them what to do. However, this will not be a long-lasting organization. When being close-minded, new ideas and improvements will not be promoted or heard creating a stale and stagnant organization.

- Micromanagement. This is one of the worst characteristics of an organization. It takes the freedom from employees in every way. This is also a sign of a lack of confidence in the employee, the manager's lack of confidence in his or her ability to manage, lack of trust and faith in the people and the organization, large egos that need to be satisfied by making certain that the manager's name is on everything, and the need to control. This is one of the most frequently encountered reasons for managers' and companies' failures. Sometimes it is justified to micromanage, to push the organization by having high expectations or when serious problems are being encountered. However, this should not be the norm nor should it continue for a long time when it does happen. When the need is there to get involved at any level, then whatever needs to get accomplished or resolved must be done, but again, this cannot be long-lasting.

- Lack of efficient tools. When employees do not have the right tools to perform their tasks, the job will not get done correctly, efficiently, or effectively. Better tools also imply that the company cares about its employees and the goals they are meant to achieve. In the end, it is the company that will win through higher efficiency, better products, a healthier working environment, and strong relationships among people at all levels of the organization.

- Unrealistic expectations and demands. Have you noticed that when a company's business is not going well, management begins to push and put undue pressure on employees to improve the situation? This can get ugly. Sometimes it is better to just stop and review the situation, gathering all the available relevant data and information to determine the causes for the company's condition. Only then should the work be done with the necessary urgency. Working a lot or working harder does not do it. It is working smart that makes the difference and creates advancements for everyone. It should be considered that the reason for the existing situation facing the company could be poor decisions made, an inefficient process, or the lack of qualified personnel in key positions.

In one of my positions as vice president, I reported to the president of the company. I had joined the company when there were fewer than 15 employees. There were not many things to disagree on. However, as the number of employees and products increased, more meetings were taking place, more issues were popping up, and more decisions needed to be made to push things forward. With this growth, there were more opportunities for disagreements and more reasons for arguments. With the president's frustrations due to product delays and employee issues, he and I began to have dis-

agreements, which led to arguments in meetings in front of other employees. These incidents used to derail the meetings, causing the attendees to freeze and not participate freely and openly since the ones arguing were the president and vice president of the company. The result was ineffective and inefficient meetings, discord among colleagues, and temporary paralysis of the entire organization, leading to the surfacing of more frustrating issues. The proper etiquette would have been for the president to take the disagreements and arguments off-line, into his office and away from the ears and eyes of the rest of the employees. He should have displayed unity with senior management, his staff, in front of the employees. The organization never recovered from some of these incidents, and attrition began.

NHF-III: Destructive Criticism

Destructive criticism of others is a sign of character weakness, inferiority complex, insecurity, or immaturity. Destructive criticism is one of the worst NHFs. It is one of the fastest ways to destroy the integrity of an individual, and when it happens frequently, it will lead to the destruction of the integrity of an entire organization. It robs the individual criticized of his or her self-esteem and confidence. It sheds doubt on the individual's thoughts and plans. It basically causes the individual being criticized to freeze, losing motivation and initiative. In addition, when destructive criticism takes place in public, in front of colleagues, superiors, or especially in front of subordinates, it could be the most humiliating experience in one's professional life.

It is important to realize that destructive criticism does not mean giving advice or trying to correct a mistake or weakness one has. It is the act of putting someone down, insulting, demeaning, and making a mockery out of that individual. The usual purpose of using destructive criticism in the workplace is to gain status or favor. Unfortunately, it is usually done at the expense of someone else. In many companies and organizations this is left unattended and usually grows to become a cultural attribute, which will eventually ruin that business entity and its business because it destroys the human component of business.

Unfortunately destructive criticism is a sign of immaturity and inexperience in dealing with others, and in the development of others. Parents can do tremendous damage, sometimes irreversible, to their children when they criticize them. The criticism does not have to be through the use of huge words or long statements. It can be as simple as saying such things as, "You're so lazy," "You can't do anything right," or "You're so stupid." Constant and repeated use of such phrases will instill that belief in the child. The same thing applies to the business environment. When someone's opinions or comments are always undermined, that person will never develop or excel. Destructive criticism is sometimes used to control and influence others to serve one's hidden agenda. It is these unethical practices that do the most damage to the character and emotional and mental health of the individual and eventually to the entire organization.

NHF-IV: Sensitivity, Anger, Emotional Ups and Downs, and Personality Conflicts

Feelings and emotions are part of being human. We all have them in varying intensities, some more than others, and some more frequently than others. Even though feelings and emotions are not physical, their stability creates a well-rounded strength in individuals. External or internal events, personal or company-related, cause individuals to experience, and sometimes display, a variety of feelings, such as emotional ups and downs, anger, and sensitivity. These are all real and very tricky to handle because they are personal and emotional in nature and require understanding, patience, support, maturity, forgiveness, and compassion. Too often these individuals are labeled as weak, unstable, unreliable, and ineffective. In many instances they are not recognized, considered for any promotions, or even invited to participate in internal or external meetings or planning sessions.

Within reasonable limits of time and effort, before judging and labeling those who display their feelings and emotions, it is important to approach and establish a dialogue, a channel of communication to reach and understand them and their total environment, the internal and external environments. Verify whether the emotional outburst is due to true instability, immaturity, or is it out of concern for people and the business. Time may heal the wounds; however, communication is critical to speed up the process since many are not capable of sharing their feelings and emotions due to the fear and stigma of being labeled as emotional or sensitive that may follow them for the rest of their careers. It is important, however, for these conditions to be contained and not allowed to spill over into other areas of the team or the organization.

Anger is one of the most, if not the most, dangerous of emotions that can be displayed in the workplace. It results in an unclear mind, unclear thinking, and the inability to make wise subjective decisions or judgments. When anger occurs it must be dealt with immediately and resolved quickly. If anger continues, the effects on the organization will be extremely negative and will get in the way of conducting business effectively. Anger must not be taken for granted or brushed aside and attributed to a multitude of excuses. Management must analyze the situation carefully to ensure that the causes are not related to the work environment, the organization, or any element of the business entity. Even if the cause for the anger is determined to be related to the business, there is no justification for the behavior to occur repeatedly in a professional, business environment. I am not suggesting that one should never, under any circumstance, get angry in the workplace. This is not realistic. However, just as for everything else, there must be a limit to the intensity and frequency of anger any one individual displays.

Personal and company factors, external and internal respectively, are reasons for personnel to display a wide range of emotions in the workplace. However, some of these are part of the individuals' character and make-up, regardless of the surrounding environment. Some are hidden, buried deep inside the individual. They will surface, however, when certain events are encountered, and when they do, the emotional floodgates open up and feelings begin to flow. These could be positive emotions in reaction to positive events or they could be negative emotions in reaction to negative events. And sometimes the positive and negative get mixed up due to misunderstandings and perceptions. It is, therefore, very important to be clear, forthcoming, and ethical.

Even though certain positive emotions are displayed by loud, continuous laughter and conversations, or by acting childish and immature, being the joker can be distracting to others. Those who are not in the same frame of mind and who want a quiet atmosphere to do their work could perceive these individuals as inconsiderate. Of course there is a limit for everything, but respect must be given to people's feelings in order to create a healthy and harmonious work environment.

However, it is the negative emotions and feelings that companies must address and pay close attention to. It is negative events that cause the negative emotions to surface and cause havoc, and those events need to be monitored and paid close attention to as well. Negative events can be external or internal, personal or work-related. Negative external events that are personal in nature could be any of the following:

- Family and marital problems.
- Illness.
- Financial difficulties.
- Social unrest.

Negative internal events that are personal in nature, on the other hand, include issues stemming from:

- The individual's character and psyche.
- Conflict with a co-worker or manager.
- Inability to perform the assigned tasks.
- Difficulty in working within the organizational structure.
- Lack of direction due to inefficient internal communication.
- Incompatibility with corporate culture, style, and policies.
- Insufficient work force.
- Difficulty fitting in with the rest of the work force.

Such events, when introduced into the daily life of an employee, can create sensitivities within the individual toward a number of things. In such a mental state, defensive behavior causes misinterpretation toward events like the following:

- Any type of critiquing, positive or negative.
- Requests to perform a new task or a task that is supposed to be performed by others.
- Focus on mistakes he or she made.
- Decisions not in line with his or hers.
- Being unintentionally left out of activities or meetings.

These events will then lead to resentments that will lead to underperformance and failure of that employee. This failure will then spill over into the employee's personal life, causing a vicious downward spiral. This downward spiral will eventually create more sensitivity and anger, causing emotional ups and downs and personality conflicts within the organization. This will be more harmful if the employee is a manager, since the behavior will influence the management style of that manager. In addition, the manager's inability to make rational and effective decisions will increase.

The issue of sensitivity and anger must be addressed immediately and with a plan of action to protect the health of the organization, its personnel, and its business. When sensitive or angry, different individuals react and behave differently. Behaviors such as revenge, physical and emotional attacks, unfair treatment, separation from the team, and rebellion will be demonstrated, all of which are harmful to the business, the organization, and most importantly to its people.

The third manager I worked for in Company SC was very capable and knowledgeable about the technology and products his organization was responsible for. His management skills, however, were less than ideal. Very emotional, firecracker-like behavior was his norm. He voiced whatever words came to his mind, from four-letter words to four-line insulting sentences. As a group, we did not know when an outburst was going to occur and for what reason. Again, we were intimidated and unwilling to make a stand or take a chance on anything. Why? Because he was promoted to this position from another in the same company, and therefore, we all thought management supported him. Two possibilities could have helped him get the promotion. Either he was calmer in his previous role, or his new role put added pressure on him, which caused him to be frustrated and temperamental. Management should have taken notice of his behavior and taken the appropriate actions before promoting him. Instead, he was assigned more responsibilities. Eventually, team members began showing signs of resentment, which led to several resignations costing the company several very qualified individuals. It was unethical for this manager to expose his team members to this emotional abuse through his behavior and verbal attacks, while management handled the matter with extremely poor etiquette.

NHF-V: Immaturity

I will address immaturity by discussing maturity. In business, maturity does not correlate to the individual's age, size, degree, or status. It is determined by the individual's emotional, mental, and spiritual condition and strength. The mature person will have the capacity to handle situations as they arise in the day-to-day operation and interactions of business and personal life. Immaturity, then, is the opposite. It reflects the shortcomings of the individual's emotional, mental, and spiritual capacity.

Maturity means doing and saying the right things at the right time to the right people. It enables one to select the proper method and time to deal with an issue, the proper etiquette to conduct one's self and business. Abilities of mature individuals include the following:

- Resolving issues through discussion and dialog.
- Choosing the right approach to deal with matters of any kind.
- Being patient.
- Making good decisions.
- Analyzing effectively.
- Leading and managing properly.

Let's not confuse maturity with conservatism. A conservative person can be mature or immature. A conservative person could make good or poor decisions and choices. However, a mature person could make conservative or liberal decisions, depending on the circumstances and the available facts. The reason for this is that maturity brings with it openness of the mind, flexibility, experience, and stability. When someone says, "The company or organization is not mature yet" or "We need more senior people to run the organization," what is being implied is that the organization needs personnel maturity at all levels before getting to profitability, growth, or whatever the goal may be. Yes, experience in running a particular type of business or in designing a certain product, for example, is needed, but if maturity is not established yet and is not at the right level, the outcome will always be less than optimum. This is one of the reasons why the high-tech industry is in the condition it now finds itself, with managers lacking maturity, leading to poor decisions. The same can very well be said about the fiasco of the dot com industry at the turn of the twenty-first century, when many young inexperienced managers made decisions about the viability of their business that were baseless and unrealistic, leading to the demise of many of those companies. Many great ideas existed then. However, to turn an idea into a profitable business, more than just ideas, money, experience, and smarts are needed. Complete and well-rounded maturity is a must-have to achieve success.

Through my years of experience in the high-tech industry, I have witnessed outcomes and results of immature behavior including the following:

- Poor management decisions, for business and personnel.
- Poor dialogue.
- Improper behavior.
- Manipulation by others.
- Rush to judgment.
- Emotional outbursts.
- Incorrect assumptions and using guesswork.
- Wrong timing in taking action, making decisions, or speaking.

Any of these outcomes can destroy a company, its business, and its relationships, not to mention that they can also lead to unethical acts and processes. Immaturity is a very dangerous characteristic for an individual at any level of the organization. Once the label is applied, rightly or wrongly, it will be very difficult to change that perception, especially within the high-tech industry, which is quite unforgiving, as I will explain in a later chapter.

NHF-VI: Greed, Jealousy, and Blame

Three of the worst possible character deficiencies are greed, jealousy, and blame. In personal life or in business, these three deficiencies cause vast and devastating damage to personnel, companies, and whole industries. As witnessed in the cases of Enron, Tyco, WorldCom, Arthur Anderson, and some financial institutions in the United States, the careers and lives of hundreds of thousands of people inside these companies, as well as outside, were destroyed because of the greed that swept over a few senior managers, so-called executives, to earn more, pocket more, and have more—much more—than others. The danger is that individuals who are greedy and jealous in the workplace are the same in their personal lives.

There is a difference between greed and the desire to make more and have more. There is a difference between jealousy and wishing for similar things others have. There is also a difference between blame and pointing out where a problem may exist. These differences are huge and must be understood and identified before making judgments about people.

Greed in the workplace is a controlling desire by individuals to earn more and have more than others, even though they may already have much more than those others. There is nothing wrong with earning more and having more or even wanting to achieve this goal. The catch, however, is that one should want to have more than he or she currently has—not more than others have; one should be concerned with oneself. It is also acceptable to want more as long as wanting more does not control one's life, actions, thoughts, and decisions. It is a matter of being content, for if there is no contentment, there will be no peace within. The lack of contentment and internal peace will lead to unethical actions and decisions and the birth of greed within.

When individual contributors get greedy, they will resort to whatever means they have to achieve their goal of having and making more. Their actions and decisions will be to achieve that end using the reasoning of "the end justifies the means." In business, one can earn more by meeting and exceeding performance expectations, taking credit for work well done, and abiding by the company's rules, policies, and procedures. When greed sets in, however, those greedy individuals will try to do the following:

- Take credit for work or ideas created by others.

- Step on others in their efforts to achieve their goals.

- Misrepresent and skew the information to their benefit.

- Hide delays or flaws in their deliverables.

- Blame others for mistakes or errors they make.

- Discredit colleagues so that credit is given to them.

When managers get greedy, the situation becomes even more dangerous because of the authority and influence they have over others. Managers will resort to the same tactics as the individual contributors, but their actions will have a much greater reach within the organization as they impose their decisions and delegate the necessary actions to their subordinates to achieve their objectives and hidden agendas. Greed is the Achilles' heel of any business or for that matter, any individual or relationship. From greed come jealousy and blame.

There are many reasons and causes for individuals to become jealous including the following:

- Someone else's office is bigger, better, or located in a nicer part of the building with a view.

- Someone else has more, makes more, or has a more senior position.

- Management likes someone else better.

- Someone else is invited and included in certain meetings or circles of the organization.

- Colleagues get well-deserved recognition, a promotion, or an award.

It seems that jealousy has become more prevalent in our society, in the workplace as well as in personal life. In many instances, a person is praised and elevated to new heights in status and responsibility, becoming famous, well-known, and sought after. However, as soon as the new heights are reached, the dismantlement of the individual commences. Efforts begin to find flaws and weaknesses in the individual's personality or character, past mistakes, family matters, secrets and so on. This happens not only to businessmen, but to politicians, actors, and musicians as well. This happens in private as well as in public settings. The only explanation I can give for this behavior is that it is due to jealousy. It seems that the time to do the digging for information about an individual should be before the new status is awarded and praises given, *not after*. When such acts occur in the workplace, distrust and defensiveness become the operating norm for the targeted individuals, leading to a tremendous waste of time and energy as they protect themselves from the attacks driven by jealousy. This is when the targeted individual can make mistakes because of lack of focus or wrong focus. True or not, jealousy is as potent a poison to any organization and business as greed is. One creates the other.

Greed and jealousy give birth to blame. Blame is a mechanism to protect oneself and cover up the truth as one tries to achieve their objective of having more and making more. Blame can be directed toward anyone or anything. Some blame their colleagues for not being able to complete their tasks; they blame their manager, their chair, or the lighting in their office. Blame is advertising a problem, whether true or not, and deflects attention away from the self. In the blame game the problem is pointed out to the wrong people, not those who should be informed. The ones who should be informed are those who are directly dealing with the problem, whether caused by them or not. Blame does not and will not resolve any problem. On the contrary, blame will create events such as the following:

- Amplification of problems.
- New problems.
- Fractures within the organization.
- Friction among teammates.
- Finger-pointing environment where no one is protected.
- Confusion as to where the attention should be directed.

- Tremendous waste of time and energy for individuals while people are running around trying to find the truth of the matter instead of working on correcting or improving matters.

It is critical for management to identify and deal with greed, jealousy, and blame and nip them in the bud before they develop into something worse. Most of the time, greed, jealousy, and blame are irreversible and those who have these deficiencies must be removed from positions of importance and possibly from the company altogether.

NHF-VII: Impatience

When a baker prepares the dough to bake bread, he lets it sit for several hours, even overnight, so that the dough rises, and the yeast takes effect. Only then will the baker form the dough to the desired shape and size and then begin baking. If this process is not followed or it is cut short, the bread will turn out flat, hard, and with less than desirable taste and appearance. It is the baker's patience that enables the process to complete itself and result in the desired outcome. Patience is needed on the part of the baker even if it means being late or earning less. The same principle applies to business in the treatment of employees. Without management and employee patience, the results for a business entity will be flat and not profitable. They will be hard and rigid because of the unrealistic demands put on personnel. The work environment will not be a pleasant one.

Patience is as great a virtue in business as it is in personal life. Patience is another sign of maturity. It means taking time and waiting for events to unfold. It requires avoiding rash, knee-jerk reactions. It is the only way to achieve success and avoid mistakes.

As I mentioned earlier, growing a business is like raising a child. One cannot rush the process, or mistakes are bound to happen. Patience is what guides the business through the various stages of growth. At the POS Company, where my manager did the project designs and drew the schematics for me, he was acting impatiently, rushing to get the job done even though there was plenty of time for me to do it and learn, under his guidance and supervision. The result was a less than optimum use of his time and a less than optimum training for me as an amateur design engineer.

Patience and persistence go hand in hand. When impatience dominates, persistence retreats and business fails. The individual will give up quickly or at the first sign of additional activity being required, rather than be patient and demonstrate persistence in keeping at the effort until completion. When a company is trying to penetrate a new market or produce a new product, persistence is one of the most important elements that will lead to success.

In the semiconductor "chip" industry, where I have spent more than 19 years, it is very rare that a chip will fully work when it first comes out of the fabrication facility. There will always be a flaw, small or large, that will cause the device to miss its intended performance specification. Many times, it would take two, three, or four tries before getting it right and having a product that could be delivered to the target customers. The prerequisites here are persistence and patience. Similarly, in dealing with customers, the first meeting never produces a commitment or an agreement on the customers' part to do business with the company trying to win their business. Several meetings, at various levels of both organizations, have to take place before commitment is made. Patience and persistence are the essential ingredients for this success. However, most companies, that is, their management, lose patience when their expectations are not met. These managers are driven by their myopic vision of seeing and meeting only the bottom line.

Yes, there is—and for that matter should be—a limit for the time it takes for results to materialize. However, patience is necessary. The employee may do everything perfectly well, but still the customer won't commit in the timeframe desired by the company trying to win the business. Engineers can be the best in their field and still experience problems in producing a flawless product with the first try. Companies must understand and differentiate between non-performance-related delays and failures versus complexities and external factors that are not in the control of the employee. Companies must appreciate the fact that customers are people as well and should not be rushed or treated any differently than internal personnel. Patience must be exercised with all constituencies of the company.

When an organization is impatient with a process or an employee to produce results, the process and the employee's performance and results can be weak, even a complete failure. In addition, employees under constant pressure to deliver with unrealistic schedules, and other indications of impatience on the part of management, will cut corners and resort to less than ideal methods to achieve the desired goals. Results of employees' impatience can include the following:

- Insufficient time for proper evaluation of various options.
- Not enough time to come up with other recommendations.
- No personal time to rest or recharge.
- Details falling through the cracks or being looked over.
- Mistakes being made.
- Frustration, creating a stressful environment.
- Short tempers.
- Finger-pointing when things don't go right.
- Decline in performance.

- Loss of business.
- Attrition.

Too much patience, on the other hand, is not the way to go either. It almost borders on a lazy, "don't-care" attitude. Results of too much patience may include the following:

- Extended and sometimes unrealistically long schedules.
- Delays to deliverables.
- Lax behavior with employees, customers, competitors.
- Too much flexibility.
- Creation of a lethargic organization.

Too much patience is just as harmful to a company as impatience. It is, therefore, crucial to find the right balance and differentiate between patience and procrastination, patience and laziness, and impatience and the desire to get the job done right.

NHF-VIII: Misuse of Rank and Seniority

None of us like it when someone "pulls rank" on us. We feel belittled and unimportant. Tremendous opportunity is missed when someone is treated with favoritism or mistreated because of his or her rank and seniority in the company.

However, pulling rank and seniority does have its time and place. When it is exercised with care, ethically and with etiquette, the result can be fruitful, leading to solid relationships and respect. Pulling rank is acceptable in certain situations such as these:

- An employee is not performing.
- An urgent matter needs to be addressed and the manager has to organize his or her team around that mission and make the necessary decision.
- A consensus is not possible or is not being reached and a decision must be made.

It is not always possible to be democratic and seek consensus when trying to take any type of action. At the proper point during the process, the decision or action must be dictated to the individual, team, or the entire organization. As bad as it may sound, this is almost like a dictatorship. Sometimes there is no time to waste especially when ample chance has been given to reach consensus. In such a case, the manager or management team must intervene and make the decision.

Even if it is not clear that the decision is the right one, due to the lack of data for example, a decision has to be made to move the organization forward, while keeping a watchful eye out to make the necessary adjustments during the process.

I call pulling rank with good intentions "innocent dictatorship." The short-term and long-term results of innocent dictatorship will be good. The person who's pulling rank, however, must explain the matter to, and make a request of, the person or persons who will perform the task, thus creating an atmosphere of cooperation. Notice that I am using the term "request" and not "order." Requests from a superior create willingness on the part of the subordinate. Orders create resistance. Whether strong or weak, it is still a resistance and it will slow down or completely derail any process, sooner or later.

On the other hand, when pulling rank is done to control, manipulate, or force one's will on others, it will create extremely negative results and alienation. In such situations, pulling rank is a sign of weakness and insecurity. Instead of the manager effectively communicating his or her point to the rest of the team and bringing about agreement with and acceptance of his or her views, the manager, in essence, uses force to impose his or her opinion on others. This will always result in ill feelings and rebellion within the organization.

A manager must explain the following to the team when he or she needs something done:

- What needs to get done?
- Why does it need to get done?
- When does it need to get done?
- Who needs to do it?

It is when the manager fails to rally the troops around the task that needs to be done that he or she will resort to pulling rank and exerting seniority. This will mark the beginning of the end of the organization's health because it is at this point that cracks begin to appear in the relationship between the manager and his or her subordinates. This action erodes the trust and the respect the subordinates have in their manager and in the foundation of the company's management in general since the manager is a representative of the company's management team. After all, these subordinates are people and have opinions and feelings about matters in their workplace as well. They want to succeed and prosper just as much as anyone else in the company. If for nothing else, the request, and not the order, must be made out of respect to them. As I have said earlier, there needs to be a two-way street mentality. In other word, respect in order to be respected.

Decisions must be made based on their merits and benefits, not according to whose favor will be won or whose feathers will be get ruffled. In an ethical environment, rank and seniority must not have an overriding influence on making decisions. Serious attention must be given to a person with high rank or seniority, but all views and opinions must be heard and evaluated. Also, when faced with making a decision, a mature person will solicit the advice of a superior or one with seniority to ensure that all aspects of the issue have been addressed and analyzed based on knowledge and experience. The reason for this is that with rank and seniority comes experience. However, when decisions are made with forceful influence from a rank and seniority perspective, it will result in ill feelings. Decisions with forceful influence will cause these kinds of results:

- Resentment.
- Favoritism.
- Rebellion.
- Double standards.
- Bad judgment due to fear of rank.

Decision makers at all levels of the organization must be encouraged to make decisions that are strictly based on the available facts and for the long-term good of the entire organization and its business. This is where the strength and ethics of management become crucial in maintaining the health and integrity of the organization and its processes.

The CEO of Company SJ was of the opinion that if we generated lots and lots of press releases, the company's stock price would go up. He was also a major stakeholder in the company and wanted to have the stock price go as high as possible. In the sixth month after going public, the company's stock price began to drop. The CEO began to get extremely edgy and began exerting his authority carelessly. At one of his staff meetings, he asked me how the press releases were coming along. I stated that we were putting out as many releases as we had news worthy of a press release. He immediately started shouting, "I want you to put out a press release, even two, every week!" I tried to explain that we did not have news that warranted that many releases and that in the long run doing so would have adverse effects on the editors who pick up these press releases and write their stories. He did not hear any of that and ordered me to do what he told me; otherwise, he would fire me. The rest of his staff, including my boss, the president, was in the room when he said this. Needless to say, the stock price never recovered, even with multiple releases per week.

NHF-IX: Prejudice and Ignorance Relative to Gender, Age and Culture

One of my passions is music. I play several instruments and sing. Many of my colleagues and friend have suggested I go into the music industry. I decided to get an evaluation and a few professional voice lessons for opera. I found an instructor who was a retired opera singer. The lessons began and were going very well. She was impressed with my range and thought I had very good potential. The lessons continued very nicely until one day the conversation led to background and she asked where I was born. I told her I am Armenian but was born in Baghdad, Iraq. "Oh my," was what she came back with. She began questioning me about my opinions about the war in Iraq, how we lived among those people, and so on. This topic began to come up at every lesson until I told her that I really was not interested in discussing politics and that this topic was affecting my singing. After that she became very critical about everything I did. Even when I had to cancel a lesson because I had the flu, she would criticize me for not being serious and tell me that I would not get anywhere with this attitude. In the end I had to stop taking voice lessons. This instructor was so close-minded and prejudiced that she could not see beyond her prejudiced opinions and views. She ignored me as a person and went from nurturing and supporting me to crushing me all in a few hours of voice lessons.

Growing up, we all were taught to be nice, respectful, and accepting of people as they are. So why can't we apply what we were taught growing up to the workplace and our professional lives? When very young, we were so open and receptive that we were carefree. We had no prejudices or hypocrisy. We had male as well as female friends, we wanted to grow up quickly to hang around the older kids, we wanted to grow up to be like our parents, we had friends with different cultural backgrounds, from different races and different countries. Somehow, sadly, change takes place and we lose the openness.

The questions to ask ourselves are: "What changed within us now that we are older?" "Where did our openness and receptiveness go?" "Why can't we interact with different types of people in our professional lives?" The answer to these questions is that as we grow older, we get exposed to external factors that influence our thoughts, opinions, and views. These external factors include people, events, and experiences. These external factors that create prejudices within us cause us, among other things, to do the following:

- Develop larger egos.
- Make inaccurate assumptions.
- Become judgmental.

- Develop prejudices.
- Become arrogant.
- Lose respect for others and for ourselves.
- Become close-minded, not receptive.
- Become unforgiving.
- Develop predefined conditions in our minds for how things should be.
- Develop favoritism.
- Develop hidden agendas.
- Misplace and lose our comfort zone.
- Become opinionated.
- Develop tunnel vision.
- Become conditional rather than unconditional with our feelings and emotions toward various issues and people.

There are opposites in everything in life—male and female, old and young, large and small, good and bad, black and white. We need to learn to accept and coexist.

Business is no longer localized. It is global, which means that we conduct business worldwide with multinational corporations run by multinational personnel. When we consider different cultures, races, and their customs and habits to be less than ours, we will also apply these views to their corporations and professional personnel. This would be the kiss of death for a business. So, we somehow develop the acceptance and tolerance to deal with various people, the multinationals, and their corporations even though in our personal lives we are not as open and accepting of these cultures. We end up eating and drinking with them as part of business interactions, being polite and courteous, even buying them gifts when we travel to meet them in their countries. Now let's ask, why are we able to treat the personnel in those multinational corporations differently than we do those we live and work with, the ones in our back yards who came from those cultures that we are now doing business with? In other words, we become hypocritical, with double standards. This is the unethical part. Remember, respect cannot be selective. Respect must be given to all who earn it. When there is prejudice, there can be no respect. One never knows when the new manager or vice president or even CEO will come from a different culture. Therefore, learning about and developing appreciation for different cultures is a must in life, especially in business life.

The same argument, if you really think about it, applies to gender and age. If we are open, we can learn tremendously from everyone, young and old, male and female just as we can from other cultures. An organization will break up quickly when different personnel are treated differently and unfairly because of their gender, age, or cultural background. Unfortunately, despite all of the equal rights policies and teachings, we still have enormous deficiencies in the way we treat gender and age. Age, for example, brings with it life's experience. It offers the understanding of how to deal with different people, different human emotions and factors, and different conditions and situations. This understanding cannot be taught in schools or by reading books and attending seminars. It is picked up along the road of growing up and living life.

Prejudice against gender, age, religion, and other cultures is in essence prejudice against people, against individuals. The cause of this prejudice, this disease, is ignorance. When individuals are uninformed or choose not to learn and appreciate others, no matter who those others are, judgments and opinions that are based on falsehood arise. The blinders will come down and a myopic vision develops, not allowing the openness needed to see the other side for what and who they are and to develop the appreciation and respect deserved. This is the reason why so many cultures have clashed and countries have been ruined. If you consider a country as a corporation, which in more ways than one it is, you will find that not everyone is a politician, not everyone is a general or a soldier, not everyone is a doctor, and not everyone is gentle or compassionate. Every type of person is needed to create the whole. The same holds true for any corporation.

My father, who was a high achiever, believed that one must be productive the entire day and, to do so, one needs to rest and recharge. To achieve this he took short power naps his entire life. It was so important to him to take those fifteen- to twenty-minute naps that only then would he really get upset if he were disturbed.

When I joined semiconductor Company SC even though I was still a member of the technical staff for the company, I now had much more customer and sales interaction, which was my objective. So there was a lot to learn and get accustomed to. I also began attending a local college pursuing a Masters degree in Business Administration, an MBA. In addition, my first son was eighteen months old at that time and tended to wake up a few times during the night, screaming his head off for food. It felt like having three jobs with overtime. However, each one was very important and satisfying in its own way

Remembering my father and how productive he was, I decided to follow in his footsteps and began taking fifteen- to twenty-minute naps during my lunch break in order to remain productive throughout my time at work, and after work as well. During my lunch break, I used to go to my car, my new Jeep Cherokee, drive it under one of the trees in the parking lot, and snooze. When I went back to my cubicle after my nap, I used to feel refreshed and would put in another six to seven productive hours after lunch. One day, when I was coming back from my nap, a co-worker noticed the imprint of my car's seat fabric on the side of my face. His comment to me was, "Had too much to drink last night?" That was the last time I took a nap. My late afternoon productivity was not as high, and I was unable to stay as late at work. Not only did the group and ultimately the organization lose some productivity, but I also lost the opportunity to more quickly advance my knowledge and skills by doing work while more rested and alert. This was an acceptable habit for the culture my father came from and I learned it from my father. It was not, and is still not, acceptable in the U.S. to take naps while at work, even during lunch. The individual who does so will be labeled lazy, or an excessive drinker, or something along those lines. In fact, the CEO of one of the largest high-tech companies fired an engineer for taking a nap at his desk during his lunch hour. The CEO did not know the engineer had worked past midnight completing a design the day before.

NHF-X: Dishonesty, Lying, Deceit, and Manipulation

Dishonesty and manipulation are as dangerous to the health of an organization as greed and jealousy are. These two sets of characteristics go hand in hand. One set will lead to the other, sooner or later. Sadly, if a person is dishonest and manipulative at work, he or she is the same, in personal life as well because being so is a character flaw, a character weakness. Dishonesty and manipulation are unethical and tear apart the fabric of a corporation, permanently damaging its integrity and reputation. These will uproot trust and cause employees, customers, partners, investors, and suppliers to question every decision, action, and communication from the company in an effort to determine whether what is being presented is true, if there is a hidden agenda. All this will cost the company time, money, and opportunity. "Treat people the same way you want to be treated" should be a saying to live by. The negative effects of this NHF reach deep into the foundation of a company and its people. Employees will have doubts about everything from business plans to decisions made, from communication memos to product schedules. Any issue becomes a significant matter for all involved when trust is broken.

Think about it—when an employee is visiting a potential client to present or introduce a new product, if nothing else, the one positive this employee has to possibly win the customer and the business is self-confidence. This is especially true during a first-time meeting with this customer. Self-confidence, however, goes down to zero when dishonesty and manipulation is detected within this employee's organization. Thoughts that might go through an employee's mind when self-confidence is lost could include the following:

- Can I trust the information I was given?
- Does the product really do all that is stated in the manual?
- Will the customer get the support needed?
- What can I commit to?
- Should I do or say…?
- Is my reputation in jeopardy?

As we all know, customers are not stupid. They are perceptive and experienced and will be able to detect the employee's discomfort. This discernment leads to more scrutiny to validate the information provided and to try to establish trust and a comfort level from which a decision can be made. Otherwise, the business will not be awarded.

The same is applicable to interactions within the company, between different groups or different individuals. All of this, however, starts and stops at the top of the company, with its management team. They set the example with their actions. Often management preaches integrity, honesty, and respect but turns around and change the rules on the fly when, say, a business transaction or a customer win is at stake. Management ends up giving excuses or changing the rules, saying things like "Let's not share our true product availability schedule," "Let's not tell the potential new hire about the fact that his boss will be removed or fired, and the new hire will have to report elsewhere in the organization or get assigned to a new position," knowing well that if the potential new hire knew this he or she would not have accepted the job. These are just a few examples of dishonesty and manipulation. Ironically, the person experiencing this may also tend to become dishonest or manipulating in nature.

What can be expected from employees when they see their managers or colleagues perform in this manner? As in a parent-child relationship, the child will imitate the parent. This could become a lifelong habit or the child will fight and change when he or she grows up. Personnel will do the same. They will be corrupted or leave as they gain experience and get exposure.

One of the statements I really dislike is "It is about perception, not reality." In other words, with this mentality, creating an illusion is acceptable. With such a statement, businesses are promoting deception, a mirage that will lead constituents in a direction they would not have been interested in taking otherwise, due to potential risks. Running a business is not a magic show. It is about hard facts and truth in presenting the products and services to all constituents, the internal and external customers of the company. It is doing the right thing in the right way.

It should be kept in mind that sooner or later, the truth will come out and the effects will be devastating to the person and the organization. Keep in mind that in most cases trust can never be reestablished, especially in the business world where strangers are collaborating in good faith to make something good out of an idea. When good intentions are met with dishonesty and manipulation, the game will be over.

Years ago, I interviewed with Company M for a marketing position. At the time, I was a vice president and was ready for the next step upward, in my career. Even though the company was of interest to me and they were in one of my favorite markets, the position was not satisfying and challenging enough. I decided to decline the offer. However, the hiring manager, who was a vice president himself, called me back and dangled a huge carrot in front of me. He said, "The company has made the decision to combine a couple of its groups to create a division, and you will be one of the prime candidates to head up the division as its general manager." He also said, "This is not a promise but a consideration." This excited me, and I was up to the challenge and willing to compete, fairly, for the general manager position. I had faith in my abilities and felt confident that I could win the position. However, I was also prepared to accept the idea of letting the better person win the position as long as the company conducted a fair evaluation. I accepted the marketing position with the understanding that I would be considered for the general manager position. After two to three weeks on the job, I found out that the decision had already been made regarding the general manager and that there was going to be no evaluation or consideration of anyone else for that position. I went home that day feeling as if I'd been clubbed on the head. Even though I kept my commitment to do the job I was hired to do, I could never overcome what had happened and I resigned. This company not only lost me, but it lost many others to this type of behavior. Now it was faced with the task of hiring and training new people, which meant time, money, and lost opportunity. In addition, by continuously having to replace personnel, more of its proprietary information was released, which made the company vulnerable to the competition since the employees it lost went to the competition. The company's reputation was tarnished and its business affected. This company no longer exists. As to the effect this incident had on my career, it was devastating. I lost time and better opportunities I was pursuing before accepting the position.

Dishonesty and manipulation can occur in many areas of business, such as accounting, recruiting, scheduling, trip reports and expenses. Enron, WorldCom, Tyco, and Global Crossing are all huge and established publicly traded companies with federal agencies overseeing their activities, yet they were able to pull off some of the most sophisticated unethical practices ever recorded in business history. Where there is a will, there is a way, and if the will is to deceive and manipulate, the way will be found. It was not only management that was involved in these companies' deceptions, but also some lower-level managers and individual contributors. It starts at the top, however, because when the head is corrupt, the rest of the body will not function properly.

The negative human factors that I believe have the most devastating adverse impact on a business have been discussed. Figure 4 below illustrates the hurricane-like force these negative human factors possess and how they are capable of destroying everything in its path, no exceptions.

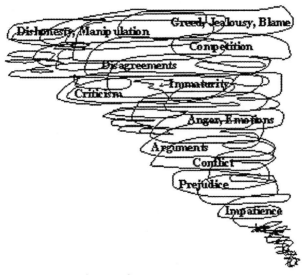

Figure 4 Destructive negative human factors

Personnel Etiquette

Fairness Is the Greatest Equalizer

Just as organizations need to keep their end of the bargain, employees, management, and individual contributors alike need to honor theirs. It is all about a two-way-street mentality. The attitude and mindset must focus on the act of giving before the act of receiving. Employees have an obligation to their employer; after all, management personnel are people, too. Employees have to acknowledge the fact that the employer has entrusted them with a specific task, which is the reason for hiring them and paying their salary. When all is said and done, employees have to take responsibility for their own actions and activities, performance and success, utilizing the tools the company provides them with to do the job as best they can. Employees' responsibilities include the following:

- Identifying problems. This is one of the most important tasks for an employee. It is the collective effort of personnel that creates success. However, it shouldn't be only problems that are brought to the table. We can all point to problems. However, identified problems must be accompanied with solutions or indication where the solutions can be found, internal or external to the company.

- Pointing out weaknesses found anywhere in the organization, in the products, in available skills, and so on. This does not only mean identifying a flaw or problem in people. It could be reorganizing a group or redefining a process, for example, that could be done more efficiently or more quickly.

- Being cooperative. Being cooperative is not just working together on projects. It also means being open and receptive, accepting the views and decisions of people inside or even outside the organization. It is perfectly OK to state one's point, give his or her views, and share opinions about various matters. However, if and when the organization does not adopt one's plan and elects to use another method, the individual cannot rebel and fight the system—he or she must go with the flow. Of course, an explanation should be forthcoming as to the reasons the organization did not select the individual's proposal. Initially one must not fight the system. Even though it is against or not in line with the employee's views, the employee must accept the decision and do the job as if everything had gone his or her way. Perhaps the time will come when the organization will recognize that the employee's views were in fact the correct ones. If it is a mature and healthy organization, it will modify the decision made and possibly adopt the employee's plan. On the other hand, the employee may find the organization's plan was the better one and thus learn from the experience.

- Being punctual. I used to tell my team members "You can arrive to work late, or you can leave early, or take a long lunch. However, you can not do any two out of the three in the same day." Even though getting the job done is not totally dependent on how much time employees spend at work, employees need to spend the appropriate time at work to complete their tasks, as well as offer support to colleagues, and build and experience teamwork.

- Being attentive. Take care of everything in the organization, from the assigned tasks to the needs of the other employees, to the working area, the facilities, the equipment and supplies.

- Helping managers achieve their goals. Good employees know that when managers accomplish their goals, it means that every team member is meeting his or her goals as well.

- Being honest and truthful. This begins as early as the first interview. Untruthful interviewees may pass the test and get the job, but sooner or later the truth will be found and the damage irreparable. If, for example, an interviewee has not had Profit and Loss (P&L) experience but says otherwise, the time will come when the P&L statement will be needed. That's when the lack of P&L experience will surface.

Interacting with others in the workplace is truly a two-way street. It is a give-and-take system. However, when colleagues, employer and employee, partners, and so on, have the capacity and willingness to give before receiving, the impact will be enormously positive and conducive to a harmonious environment. Total prosperity will be attainable for everyone. Employees must give to and take care of their organizations and their managers, just as the organization and managers must give to and take care of their employees.

The best way for companies to take care of themselves is by using practices like these:

- Creating the right policies and procedures to conduct business.
- Recognizing a job well done.
- Having the right management team, structure, style, capability, and characteristics.
- Mentoring and training new and entry-level employees.

- Offering growth opportunities for all employees, including managers.
- Offering fair compensation and benefits.
- Setting up the right organizational structure. This will enable employees, including management, to do their jobs more efficiently and meet the company's goals and objectives.
- Providing tools to aid the employees in efficiently and effectively achieving their objectives.
- Creating comfortable facilities. Employees spend more time at work than they do in their own homes. It is, therefore, most important to offer as comfortable and beautiful a facility and campus to employees as possible. This includes having good-sized cubicles, clean and well-maintained grounds, comfortable furniture, and so forth. This environment will also create a favorable impression of the company when its constituents are visiting.

In addition to taking care of the company and the managers they work for, employees must take care of themselves. They need to develop and maintain a balanced life. They have to have rich, healthy, and exciting lives outside of work. The balancing factors may include family, friends, recreation, sports activities, exercise, and hobbies. Not only do the employees need to work to establish this balance, but also companies and management must promote and encourage it to ensure that the employees are healthy, happy, and productive. For example, if managers notice some of their employees spending excessive amounts of time at work, that is, always working fourteen or fifteen hours a day and spending weekends at work as well, they need to get involved. An employee's condition should never reach a burnout stage because it will be too late by then to turn things around quickly. The turnaround and recovery efforts will take too long, costing the employee and the company dearly.

Professional Conduct

One's Conduct Is a Reflection of One's State of Mind

At Company SC, I attended a management seminar organized and offered by the company itself. This event was taking place after the project status meeting where my manager had taken credit for my successes in aiding the company's penetration of a new market and winning the largest customer in that market. One of the speakers was an executive vice president (EVP) who really impressed me with his demeanor and the theme of his speech. He talked about trust and what trust does to businesses and individuals and why. At the end of the seminar, during the happy hour gathering, I approached this EVP and asked him, "How can one establish trust after going through events that rob the individual of his or her ability to trust others, be they strangers or colleagues?" His answer is still with me until today and it has shaped the way I have conducted myself since then. He said, "You have to approach people with the opinion that they are good." He continued, "and you begin chipping away, if you have to, at the trust you have for them after they prove themselves untrustworthy through their actions and conduct!"

To start from a mistrusting position is an uphill battle and a tremendous waste of time and energy for both parties. Approaching people with distrust will cause them to keep their distance, especially if they detect your disposition. You will have to spend energy trying to find proofs that they are trustworthy or otherwise. In all cases, it is a losing proposition for growth and success.

What I mean by "professional conduct" is the way in which every employee treats his or her employer and colleagues, in his or her professional life, at work and outside of work. Such treatment is productive and energizing when guided by good ethics and etiquette. It provides direction and meaning to the individuals and business to collaborate and instill camaraderie. Things begin to happen out of care and the desire to do good, leading to growth, prosperity, and success.

When a company hires us, the company is handing to us the responsibility to develop and help grow a product or an idea in its infancy. So why can't we apply the same thought and action to this as we would to any situation that requires care? Think about it—by helping the company, your employer, you are helping many people, including yourself, to succeed. Whether the product or idea is formally handed to you or you see it from a distance, efforts must be made to rescue or support that business, product, or idea to avoid failure. When someone says, "It's my baby" when talking about a project or product, this indicates that care must go into making the project or products successful for the business entity.

Having the ability to make decisions about behavior and manners is only one in a long list of requirements that make up the landscape of professional conduct. This *professional conduct landscape* is all-encompassing and includes the following skills and knowledge:

- How to make decisions, when and with whom to share those decisions, how to explain and communicate the decisions.

- How to form opinions and views about different matters, and, similarly, how, when and with whom to share and communicate these opinions. To build an opinion or a viewpoint about a concept, process, or any other matter, begin with a totally willing and open mind to receive all possibilities and options, including those that one might have disagreed with. Remember to be flexible in your opinions. Stand by your opinion but also be open and ready to change it. To do so, you must acquire a full understanding and appreciation for the issues surrounding ideas, your own and the others. Try to understand and evaluate the issues from others' points of view. It is most important to know when to soften your position and back down and when not to. Either way, respect should never be lost or taken away from those who have or believe in the other idea.

- How to stand up for what you believe in without damaging your integrity and the integrity of the establishment or any of its processes. This means to know how, when, and to whom to say no or to disagree without creating conflict and disruption. This means not just saying things that others want to hear. In other words, don't be a yes-person. To say what you believe in, you must make sure that your intentions and reputation are impeccable so that you are believable and are taken seriously. Again, you must have full knowledge and understanding of the issues before making any strong and decisive statements and taking one position or the other. One should not appear to be wavering from one viewpoint to another.

The Wisdom in What I Learned

Excellence Will Neither Justify Nor Nullify Misbehavior

Ethical People Respect and Promote Equality

Fairness Is the Greatest Equalizer

One's Conduct Is a Reflection of One's State of Mind

Emotions Come from Being Human and Caring

Emotions Are Destructive When Born Out of Insecurity

Chapter Four

Management

When the Head Is Unhealthy and Malfunctioning,
The Entire Body Will Break Down and Malfunction

The character of a company's management team is a reflection of the company itself, its personality and its maturity. The management team is the head of the corporate body and what the head stands for, thinks, behaves, and understands will mold and shape the corporation. Since management is made up of personnel, again, we come right back to the foundation of any company, its people.

For any business entity, these are the initial and primary goals for creating the management team:

- To choose the right personnel to build the management team with, individuals who have high professional and personal ethics, maturity and experience.

- To define the right management structure to achieve the goals set forth by the business entity.

In the high-tech industry, for example, many companies were established, capital raised, products defined, and personnel hired only to see many of them collapse and disappear or get the management team replaced to revive the company and help it survive. Why? The answer is "because of a poor management team and/or structure." The problem is so widespread that many of the startup companies have the investors, venture capitalists, on their management team. The problem is so serious that an enormous amount of effort has been spent on the topic. Places where management topics have been addressed include the following:

- Articles have been published in industry publications, newspapers, and business journals, all pointing to the fact that better management is needed and that management is weak, even lacking.

- Many business schools have added new courses and curriculum to address this deficiency.

- Entire industries have emerged to address the issue, with the management consulting and executive search firms helping companies identify and select the right management talent.

- Companies have encouraged their top performers to go back to school and obtain an MBA degree to refine their skills and prepare them for management positions.

- Internal and external seminars have been given, teaching and training employees in management skills.

However, after years of effort, the problem of poor or lacking management in all types of companies and industries persists. The reason for this persistence is that most of these topics and efforts listed above address the issue of management from a tactical, technical, and functional point of view, while overlooking the core requirement of the management function. That core is human skills and the ability to appreciate and handle the human component that makes or breaks a good manager. After all, it is people who are doing the managing and it is people who are being managed.

To a large degree, the ability to manage is innate. Not every management trait can be taught or studied. Managing a process or activity such as designing a computer can be taught or acquired with practice and experience. Of course, one must have the ability to multitask and be organized to succeed in this area. However, the "how to" of management is the act of managing the people and their activities within a larger structure. How skillfully this is done makes the difference in the long-term success and growth of a company.

The hard truth of the matter is that the mere fact that a person is a manager or executive and is knowledgeable in the area the company is competing in does not make that person right for the position, nor does it render the person capable of being a complete manager. A person who is a complete manager is one with the right blend of professional and personal experience, that is, functional and tactical skills in his or her profession and a rich life experience with an ethically solid mental and moral capacity.

Of course, managers must have the necessary training, education, and experience to perform their functional responsibilities, such as marketing, sales, or engineering. However, management is not a science. It is being in touch with the pulse of the organization and its personnel for which the individual is responsible. There are many factors that go into the makeup of a good manager. Figure 5 shows qualifications that must be present in a person to be a good manager.

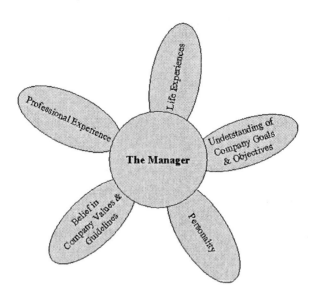

Figure 5 Required qualifications for a good manager

The qualifications of a good manager are as follows:

- Personality. The right personality for the particular company, its current situation. The personality needed could be that of someone who is an extrovert, serious, firm, hands-on, and so forth.

- Professional experience. This refers to good and bad incidents that shaped the individual's character in work-related environments.

- Life experience. This refers to good and bad incidents that shaped the individual's character in non-work-related environments: family, home, friendships, or sports.

- Compatibility with company values and guidelines. Are the manager's values in line with those of the company's?

- Compatibility with company goals and objectives. Can the manager understand the company's goals and be able to meet and deliver the company's requirements?

Different levels of management will require the individual to have more of one factor than the other, but the combination of these five factors shown in Figure 5 must be present. The right combination of all these factors will propel the manager and his or her organization to new heights.

Management Ethics

Know When to Manage and When to Delegate

As vice president of worldwide marketing and sales for Company OK, I managed a large group of professionals around the globe. Every one of them was an above-average performer with exceptional knowledge of his or her particular area of responsibility and region. Two characteristics of my management style were (and still are): first, to be hands-off, not to micromanage; and second, to take care of my team members' professional and personal needs. I wanted to build a team that had respect for each other, got along, and enjoyed each other's company. Disagreements and arguments at the professional level were perfectly acceptable, but there was no tolerance of confrontations and personal attacks. However, I began noticing a decline in the performance of two key team members. After some monitoring, the truth was uncovered. One was selling Amway products on the side on company time while the other was consulting for another company, also on company time—my time, the group's time. These acts not only affected me personally, but they also disturbed the harmony of the entire group. The delays in projects that we thought were due to difficulties were actually the result of neglect and game-playing. These delays had chipped away at the credibility of the group as marketing, technical support, and sales organizations. This was so serious to my group and me that I was criticized for being too hands-off and soft in my style of management. This was the view because I had obliged those two individuals by giving them a lot of flexibility in performing their duties and achieving their goals since both were going through some difficulties in their personal lives. Even though I had a gut feeling about the reasons for the problems, I did not act on those feelings out of care for those individuals and their families. I should have paid more attention to the needs and feelings of the rest of my group. On the other hand, the unethical conduct of these two individuals caused so much damage to the rest of their teammates and to the organization as a whole that the effects lingered for many months after they were let go. It is very difficult and time-consuming to rebuild broken trust. In this example, it is clear that decisions made by those two employees and by me affected the organization in different but adverse ways even though the intentions were different. Both of our actions and decisions compounded the results.

In management, power and authority must not be exerted down through the organization strictly to push through a personal agenda, views, or unsupported opinions. This is also referred to as "pulling rank." Instead, the roles must be reversed with the subordinates and more junior managers where the question asked must be, "What can I, the manager, do or influence for my team members, the employees of my organization and my company so that we can succeed?" In other words, "What obstacles do I need to remove for my team to achieve success?" Before acting, managers must answer the following questions:

- What decisions need to be made?
- Whom and how do these decisions help?
- Whom do these decisions affect and how do they affect them?
- Is this the right time for these decisions to be made?
- Are the appropriate skill sets, experience, and background available within the organization to make the right decisions?
- Are the appropriate skill sets, experience, and background available to carry out the execution of these decisions?

The answers to these and other questions must be fully weighed and evaluated. All pros and cons must be considered before moving forward. When managers manage with this in mind, their team members will do the same, creating an atmosphere of cooperation and support. What this means is that managers must do more than coexist with their team members. They must feel what they feel, experience what they experience, going through the ups and downs of the processes and the business cycles together. This helps to create unity. Remember this: "When acting ethically and with proper etiquette, employees will work with ease." "When management does not have hidden agendas, the employees will not feel pressured or threatened."

In addition to managers' functional responsibility, managers' duties toward their team members—the managers' "Dos"—include these activities:

- Ensuring the well-being of their employees, their employees' overall balanced existence. Encouraging their employees to have a balance between work, friends, family, activities, and hobbies. Ensuring that burnout conditions will not exist anywhere in their organization.
- Selecting and retaining good and healthy employees.
- Delegating the right task at the right time to the right person.
- Being a facilitator for their team members to help them achieve their goals and objectives. When each team member achieves his or her objectives, so does the rest of the organization. Therefore, some of the most important roles a manager has to perform for his or her team members are to train, mentor, remove obstacles, mediate, protect, and guide.
- Encouraging employees to make decisions and think outside the box, to come up with new ideas and new ways of doing things, to be creative.

- Acknowledging in writing a job well done, making sure to copy other members of management. Awards are another way of recognizing good performers. Many companies consider this an unnecessary expense that the company cannot afford. However, the opposite is true. The monetary cost of these awards is minuscule compared to the benefits the company will reap from increased productivity and the commitment of those employees who are rewarded. It will create an environment where the employees themselves, without management's imposition, will always push the bar higher.

- Giving credit when and where credit is due.

- Critiquing from a positive perspective.

- Setting goals for the team members, monthly, quarterly, and biannually or annually. These will be the short- and long-term goals for the individuals to manage and guide their activities toward the organization's goals, ensuring alignment with the rest of the team members. These should be measurable goals with precise due dates and deliverables. Team members must know what is expected of them. They should also be aware of what their manager's goals and objectives are, set by his or her manager. This will ensure that everyone is marching toward a common goal for the organization.

- Encouraging team members to improve themselves.

- Protecting the team members' dignity.

On the other hand, there are activities that a manager's role toward his or her team does not include—the managers' "Don'ts":

- Don't manage every minute of a team member's time and every activity. In other words, don't micromanage.

- Don't criticize, especially in the presence of subordinates, colleagues or other managers. When a team member makes a mistake, it is the manager's role to mentor and guide. However, the manager must pay attention and monitor the development of the individual to make sure he or she is learning and advancing, and not repeatedly making the same mistake that may be causing the criticism. In all cases, the treatment must be in private to protect the individual's self-esteem and dignity, in addition to preserving his or her colleagues' respect. The privacy with which such matters must be handled maintains and protects the health and integrity of the entire organization. Most importantly, it will protect the relationship between the manager and the subordinate. When team members see that those who sometimes make mistakes are not punished or ridiculed, they will become more averse to making decisions and taking calculated risks. This will in turn facilitate creativity and progress. Again, there must be a limit to the mistakes forgiven or overlooked.

- Don't suppress and restrict team members' freedom to think, experiment, and develop themselves, within appropriate boundaries and agreed-upon guidelines.

- Don't take credit for a team member's success.

- Don't continually delegate his or her own responsibilities to team members so that the manager can pursue his or her own personal plans, whatever the plans may be.

- Don't pit teams or team members against each other, creating a confrontational environment.

- Don't use team members to achieve personal agendas.

Figure 6 summarizes the manager's dos and don'ts in an illustration that demonstrates how the manager's behavior and management style impacts team members and the rest of the organization. The figure shows a thermometer depicting an organization's health demonstrated through the temperature readings. The right side of the thermometer shows the organization becoming feverish as a result of poor management, which is the outcome of micromanagement; criticism, and the rest of the items listed previously—the don'ts of the manager. On the left side of the thermometer, the fever drops and the organization regains its health with good management such as encouragement, facilitation, and the other items previously listed—the dos of the manager. The bottom line is that the manager's actions and decisions have far-reaching positive or negative effects on any type and size of organization, its personnel, and its business potential.

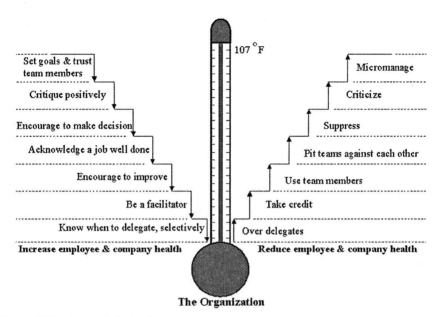

Figure 6 The dos and don'ts for managers

At Company OK, one of the hardest decisions I had to make in my professional career was to resign that position because of fundamental differences between my values and the management style and values of the president of the company, my boss. Several weeks after I had left the company, I met for a happy hour drink after work with one of the managers who had reported to me. What he told me during our conversation still resonates with me. He said, "Your problem, Vahé, was that you took care of your employees too much!" He continued by saying, "You went out of your way to accommodate your employees' needs." I did not know how to take it, or what to make of that statement. I always felt and thought, and still do, that you take care of those you are responsible for, those who are doing good things for your organization and for the rest of the company, of course, within acceptable limits. Later on, I realized what he meant. I remembered an incident when the daughter of one of the members of my group was going to turn one year old while he was on a business trip with me. He really wanted to be there for her birthday party. I had him fly back home for the birthday and then fly back out the day after to meet up with me, all at the company's expense. However, I was not met with the same treatment from this individual. While he was working for me he was also doing consulting work for another company on the side. He was fired. However, the events of the following eight months made me realize and understand the lesson in what I had done, in that I was correct in the way I had managed my organization. Eight months after my departure, only 30 percent of the personnel I managed remained with the company.

Management Etiquette

Excellence Neither Justifies Nor Nullifies Corruption

The president of Company SJ, where I was the vice president of marketing, managed by confrontation. He would, for example, allow engineering to complain to him about marketing, and sales to complain about customer support, and so on. He would then go to the head of, let's say, marketing, and inform him that engineering was unhappy with the marketing group's performance and that he needed to come down on certain members of the marketing team so that they would contribute more, and so on. The result was a fragmented organization.

Needless to say, the company did not survive. Neither did the president. This type of management was conducive to nothing but confrontation, finger-pointing, distrust, and resentment.

Of course, the senior manager of a company, the president or CEO, must listen to issues and problems raised by different parts of the organization. However, the action then should be to encourage different groups and departments to work out their differences on their own, without involving the entire company or pulling in other parts of it. If, after trying to resolve the issues among themselves, matters do not change for the better, intervention at that time will be appropriate to resolve the problems whatever they are and wherever they may exist.

At the top of the list of questions that should be asked and answered when organizing and establishing a business entity is the question of management. Does the organization have the right management team and management structure? Without the right management team and structure that will utilize the expertise and experiences of the entire team, no company can succeed. Keep in mind what I stated earlier: "If the head is dysfunctional and does not work well, the rest of the body will malfunction."

The first question that must be answered when setting up the management team and structure should address the top two management positions at any company, positions of CEO and chairman of the board. How can there be proper management practice when the same individual holds the chairmanship of the board of directors and the CEO position? Most companies in most industries follow this practice, which to me does not make sense. The chairman of the board of directors is the head of the board of directors. The CEO of the company reports to the board of directors. There seems to be a conflict of interest here.

How can the same individual be the head of the board of directors as well as be the one who manages and oversees the CEO's performance when he is the CEO? It is best to have different individuals hold the CEO and the board chairman positions so that there will be proper accountability for each position.

Management is such a vital part of creating a successful business that companies must do everything possible to recruit, retain, and groom good managers. Even though it seems easier and quicker to hire managers from other companies that may already have the knowledge and experience needed, growing managers from within, from the company's ranks, offers many advantages. The most important of these advantages is the positive effects on employee morale. This act demonstrates to the employees that good performance can earn them promotions and advancements. In addition, it reflects that the company does take care of its own, its stars. The benefits the company will gain from promoting managers from within basically builds on the chosen individual's knowledge of every aspect of the company. Usually employees' knowledge of their company includes these aspects:

- Culture.
- Products.
- Markets.
- Customers.
- Competitors.
- Internal systems.
- Internal processes.
- Strengths.
- Weaknesses.
- Policies and procedures.
- Personnel.

However, companies must be very careful and thorough in evaluating the individual for a potential management position, making sure that the person is ready in every way to be a manager, a leader. Otherwise, the individual is set up for a sure failure that could adversely affect the individual's career.

The act of selecting managers must not be a popularity contest. As I mentioned earlier, promoting employees from within is very positive for the company and its employees, their morale, commitment, and dedication to excellence in their work. However, if the promotion is premature and untimely, the result will be devastating to the individual and the company as a whole. Premature promotions to management positions create an immature organization and an immature company. When a company is labeled as immature, it is actually a reference to its management and sometimes it is a reference to its processes. It is a reflection of management's lack of personal and professional maturity. Before promoting an individual to a management position, the company's management must agree that the candidate for a manager's position has to have the ability and desire to perform the following functions:

- Adhere to solid ethical standards.
- Use proper etiquette.
- Manage people.
- Manage processes.
- Manage systems.
- Spend more time in meetings.
- Develop strategies and think strategically.
- Deal with and be involved in implementation details.
- Progress, advance, and grow in all areas.
- Be compassionate.
- Be able to be tough when necessary.

These are the basic management tools. The first two items above are "must haves" to become a manager; otherwise, even if all the rest of the listed items are present, that individual must be passed on. If too many, say three or four, of the rest of the points are weak or not present in the individual, the timing of the promotion must be reevaluated. If, on the other hand, all of the above abilities are validated and are present within the individual, the promotion is appropriate and should be made. Of course, no individual will excel in all of these items 100 percent, but as long as the basics are there, the rest can be acquired.

The company must then mentor and monitor the new manager in his or her performance and progress. It is to the benefit of new managers and to the entire organization, at all levels, to monitor and evaluate managers, their management style, their results, and the atmosphere they create. This includes paying attention to the manager's behavior in public, in business events, and in meetings. Usually, the way managers conduct their personal lives is a good reflection of their management style and how they conduct themselves professionally. Values and habits, good or bad, come into play, including being supportive, understanding, forgiving, cooperative, collaborative, or being egotistic, selfish, confrontational, secretive, and manipulative. These and many other attributes can have a tremendous effect on the environment. The presence or absence of the basic management tools listed above becomes even more critical when the person is an executive, a chief executive officer, a CEO, for example. What is the role of executive officers, after all? It is to manage people ethically and move them toward a vision. If the ability and desire to manage people ethically is not 100 percent present, that executive officer has no business being in that position.

Again, I repeat, management is not a science. Many times during the course of conducting business, decisions must be, and are, made from the gut. Sometimes managers must follow their intuition when making certain decisions. Information is not always available, not always accurate, and does not always cover all possibilities. Therefore, shooting from the hip sometimes becomes a necessity. To avoid the shot taking out a team member, colleague, or an entire group, the manager's intentions and ethics, as well as professional and life experiences, must be sound. "Gut-feel" decision-making should not be relied on all the time. Some like to call it a calculated risk decision. To me it is all the same. If there is risk, then there is the unknown and when there is an unknown, then there is some information that is not available. If this is the case, the manager, after exhausting all other options, must utilize his or her experience and follow the gut feel to reach a decision to move the business forward, allowing the necessary adjustments to be made on the fly, during the process. If this is not done, then there will be a rigidity and stagnation.

One may wonder how this "gut feel" is developed and where it comes from. The answer is from experience, life experience as well as professional experience. Some may argue that one is more important than the other, but I believe that, to manage successfully, life experiences come first in importance. One has to know how to deal and interact with different people, different situations, and different environments. One can study and learn how to read financial statements, how to cut costs, or manage a process. However, the intangibles of management come from life experience. Since individuals will be the ones carrying out plans and running processes, it becomes apparent that knowing how to handle people, where no two are alike, is the priority, and that comes from life experience.

However, an important aspect of management is to build structure and create process to conduct and manage the business. The reason for companies to put a management structure in place is so that various departments and all constituents know who to go to. Otherwise it will be a chaotic operation where many things will end up falling through the cracks. Simple decisions will end up costing time and effort when done in a void. Personnel at all levels must follow the reporting structure put in place to ensure efficiency. Imagine if a vice president bypasses his direct report, the director let's say, and goes directly to the manager and a decision is made—even though the director is available. Sometimes this happens and should happen, but it should not be a common occurrence. If continued, it will offend the director and render him obsolete.

I worked for Company AT as vice president and general manager. As I was new to the company and its products, my manager used to be involved quite a bit with the daily activities, giving me time to come up to speed on all product and customer issues. I welcomed this and worked diligently to come up to speed as quickly as possible so that my manager was freed to perform his own duties. In time I gathered the necessary knowledge to run my group and was beginning to contribute to the company in my capacity. However, I did become aware of some decisions being made in the background regarding issues related to my area of responsibility. I found out that one of my direct reports insisted on continuing to go to my manager and bypassing me. I let it go for some time hoping that this was out of habit rather than intent. I was wrong. This activity continued.

Finally, I approached my team member and asked him why he continued to go around me to my manager. His reply was, "I always went to him." I told him that now that I was here to manage the group and its activities, I would like for him to come to me first and if it was determined that I cannot help or need more info, then we could decide whom to consult. He took this as being controlled and restricted and was very unhappy about the mode of operation. I did explain that I needed him to come to me so that I would be informed of the issues he is facing and be involved in the decision-making process with him working as a team. None of this registered with him and his behavior continued. However, what was worst was that my manager condoned this mode of operation, and this completely disabled me and eventually led to my inability to effectively manage my team. Even though I did go to my manager several times and request him to ask my team member to come to me first, my requests fell on deaf ears.

The Wisdom in What I Learned

When the Head Is Unhealthy and Malfunctioning, the Entire Body Will Break Down and Malfunction

Know When to Manage and When to Delegate

Excellence Will Neither Justify Nor Nullify Corruption

Chapter Five

Communication

One's Conduct Is One's Most Accurate Form of Communication

There are many forms of communication, verbal, physical, silent, written, and so on. However, the two most powerful forums used in business communication in my opinion are collateral material and meetings. Collateral materials are those documents that describe, guide, and protect the business, its people, and constituents. Collateral material includes business plans, financial statements, product manuals, and other documents. Meetings also vary in scope, size, frequency, and purpose and include customer meetings, product review meetings, strategy meetings, and so on.

I selected these two methods of communication because they can facilitate success when done correctly and ethically. But they can also be easily used for self-serving purposes and produce unethical outcomes.

All the skills, experience, plans, intentions, policies, and procedures will go to waste and be rendered worthless if not communicated to the right personnel effectively, in the right way and in a timely manner. People cannot read minds nor should they. They can assume, guess, and pretend they know and understand, all of which are dangerous to any company, its business and its employees.

Consider this. Everyone loves music and praises it for being the international language. Music is a form of communication that will enable the creation of unity, and understanding among different people and countries. Why should communication be any different in the business world? It should not be. Communication should be to business as music is to the world. It must be used to create unity and understanding.

Communication Ethics

Honest and Open Communication Is a Sign of Confidence

When I worked for Company OK as vice president of marketing and sales, my organization was not yet fully staffed. However, communications with the customer base regarding product development status and schedule had to take place. I took it upon myself to communicate with all customers by personally sending emails to each of them, giving them updates about our progress, milestone achievements, and/or setbacks in product development. Since Company OK was new in this market segment, I had to establish confidence and credibility with the target customers.

At the right point in time, when I had a good level of confidence in our ability to meet our product introduction schedule, I informed all customers of the schedule. They were skeptical since our product was unique and none of our competitors had it. This did not shake my confidence. My plan was to demonstrate our product at the most important trade show for our industry; some of our key customers would be invited to attend the demonstration.

Two of the most important customers scheduled appointments with us to view the demonstration at our private suite. They came, of course, at different times. They could not believe that we actually met our commitment. One of these customers was one of the largest high-tech companies in Germany. The director of this company, after viewing the demo, looked me in the eye and said, "I did not believe you were going to achieve this. I have never experienced anything like this. I am impressed and I will do business with you." I could've jumped through the roof with joy for we had done it. We kept our promise, kept the customer informed, and established our credibility. This happened with several other companies that we had kept abreast of our progress and accomplishment. We not only won these customers with our first product, but also we were successful in winning their business with our next products as well. On a personal level, I was able to maintain my relationship with these customers even after I left Company OK and still correspond with many of them to this day.

When we communicate, we are actually directing energy contained in our voices and words at other people. Notice that it is people and not things that are the recipient of our words and the energy these words carry because we seek a reaction or a response from those recipients. We seek positive verbal or physical response. The type of response will depend on the type of energy contained in our voices, words, and body language. We communicate because we want to get something done, something achieved. Communication can be conducted verbally, in writing or with the body. We communicate with each other to satisfy our need to be heard and to be connected to our counterparts. We can choose to have positive communication or negative ones. We can lie and cheat or be honest and truthful. We can be pleasant and joyful or be angry and grumpy. It is up to us to choose the type of communication we want to have with others. However, with a foundation built on high ethical standards, there can be only one form of communication, a positive one. It is through ethical and open communication that there will be growth, progress, prosperity for all and the resolution or elimination of problems. Positive communication produces these outcomes:

- Understanding of others is achieved.
- Connection with others is created.
- Knowledge is shared and spread.
- New opinions are formed.
- New ideas are created.
- Conflicts are resolved or avoided.
- Errors are caught.
- Errors and mistakes can be corrected.
- Dangers are avoided.
- Improvements are made.
- Growth and prosperity are achieved.
- Unity is established.

Think about it—all of the issues, difficulties, and problems addressed in previous chapters can be resolved through ethical, effective, positive, and open communication. In addition, it is communication that facilitates success and progress in business. Communication is vital. It brings the human touch, the human factor, to the surface and to the forefront. When the human factors are ethical, there can only be progress. Even "silent communication" can be utilized to make a statement or convey a message. A look or a gesture is sometimes more powerful than words and is a form of communication. Communication does not require loud voices or constant chatter to be effective.

Meetings

Communication Is Business Music

Whenever two or more people gather, a meeting is taking place. You can call it anything you want, visiting or getting together, but the bottom line is that a meeting—professional or social—is taking place. In personal life and in business, meetings are vital. Without meetings, nothing will get done, no one will succeed, and chaos will rule. In the workplace, meetings communicate information that is vital to the efficient functioning of the company, such as the following:

- Plans.
- Updates.
- Progress.
- Problems.
- Setbacks or failures.
- Organizational structure issues.
- Activities and action items.
- Opinions, views, and decisions.
- Explanations and clarifications.
- Solutions.
- Information.
- Process.

Figure 7 shows the direct relationship between topics communicated and the level of productivity in a company. As employees gain access to more information, they become more informed, acquiring the ability to make educated decisions leading to higher productivity and eventual success.

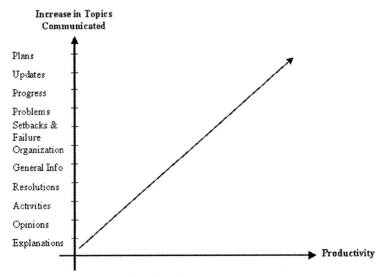

Figure 7 Topics communicated and productivity

All the topics listed on the vertical axis must be communicated regularly to create an organization with high productivity. The type of topics communicated will vary slightly from one company to the other and from industry to industry. Nevertheless, the common thread is that communication of relevant information must take place.

However, sometimes meetings are a waste of time! Why? Because they are not prepared and conducted properly. Just as one can't have a tea party without the tea, one cannot have a meeting without the right intentions, the right people, and the right and true information. Meetings are so easily called that sometimes they are more of a waste than not. Some individuals or groups even use them to push their hidden agendas and plans. This is when meetings become unethical. Communication and meetings can, therefore, cause negative as well as positive results. Always remember that a meeting is to bring people together in an effort to ethically cooperate and collaborate for the good of the entire company.

Business Collateral

Be True to Yourself

Another form of communication for a business entity is through its business collateral and documentation. Every company must communicate to its employees the value of documentation and train them on how to create the necessary documents that are pertinent to their specific function and organization. Again, for these documents to be effective, their contents must be ethical and accurate. Usually the inaccuracies are unintentional; nevertheless, the effects can be very damaging. On the other hand, when the inaccuracies in the contents of documents are intentional, the result will definitely destroy the integrity of the business and its employees, leading to the sure demise of the entity unless these intentional inaccuracies are caught and corrected in time.

Unintentional inaccuracies are due to inexperience, oversight, or plain honest mistakes. Usually the negative effects of unintentional inaccuracies are relatively easy to correct and reverse. However, inaccuracies due to the lack of experience are more serious; for example, too much or too little information, early pricing, or premature product availability dates.

On the other hand, intentional inaccuracies are the unethical and most damaging of acts in business collateral preparation. Intentional inaccuracies can occur in any document and for any number of reasons:

- Business plans—to get funds or budget for a project that would otherwise be declined if the real data were presented.

- Financial statements—to increase the valuation of the company or raise its stock price.

- Product development plan—to cover up delays or flaws in product development due to lack of expertise.
- Sales plans and forecasts—to ensure higher commissions and job security or to increase the company's valuation and stock prices.
- Memos and plans—to gain a better position or the upper hand over others; the game of politics.

There are many reasons for these and other types of documents to be affected by poor ethical standards. However, when documents have flawed information, the decisions they produce will also be flawed, eventually leading to the demise of the business, and, in turn, the individuals who devised them in the first place. What goes around comes around.

Working for Company OK, I spent three years building, from scratch, a very powerful and successful worldwide marketing and sales organization. At the end, I departed because my values and principles did not coincide with those of the president. At the beginning of my second year with the company president who had hired me resigned. A new one was hired to replace him. At the end of my second year, product delays began to mount, engineers were frustrated, customers were getting impatient, and non-engineering personnel were getting weary. I kept asking for information from the head of engineering and the president of the company, who was still very much involved in the product development activities, but none was forthcoming. One of the marketing and sales policies I had put in place was to keep the customers informed of any progress or delay and keep communicating with the customers. The delays were so great that when the truth came out, it was too late to reverse course and keep customers from going to the competition. The president of the company had ordered the engineers not to share their findings about new product flaws with the marketing and sales organization, especially with me, since he knew I would not stand for misleading the clients or the parent company's upper management.

Ten months after I departed, the president of the company, with whom I had my differences, was fired. Six months after that, the company was disbanded and ceased to exist. In this case, the problem was at the very top, the head of the organization. The president overrode the decisions made by the head of engineering to communicate the findings, rendering him obsolete and lacking clout with his team. In addition, since the product development was still not progressing according to plan, information was kept from my team, the marketing and sales organization. Having this information was critical to customers' decision making as they developed their own product plans. This unethical management and communication style not only resulted in a lawsuit by one of the company's customers, but also it adversely affected the lives of everyone in the company and was the sole cause of the company's demise.

Communication Etiquette

Meetings

*The Wise Person Is One Who Knows
What to Say, When to Say It, Whom to Say It to,
How Much to Say, and How to Say It*

In my first managerial position with Company SC, I was given the task of helping the company penetrate a new market and win the largest customer in that market. A little more than a year later, my activities had secured a "make-or-break" meeting between my company's management team and the largest customer's management team in Las Vegas during the Consumer Electronics Show. My excitement level was so high and my desire to close this win was so strong that I could almost taste it. I kept on talking, pitching and selling this customer's executive the values and benefits of our solution and of working with us.

When the meeting was over, we all got up and began walking to our suite where we had a demonstration of our solution prepared for this executive. My manager and I were at the rear of the group, and he was right in front of me when he turned and looked me in the eye and said, "I wish you knew when to keep your mouth shut." I was dumbfounded, but he was right. I talked so much that I did not leave enough time for the customer's executive to talk so that we could get a better insight into their business and how to strategize and solidify our hold on winning their entire business. This was a missed opportunity caused by my overzealous behavior and talkativeness.

One of the most important qualities of an organization, large or small, is disseminating information in a timely manner. This includes internal as well as external communications, even though internal communication is where it must start. Ask anyone—a recruiter, manager, customer, investor, partner, or anyone who is associated with a business entity and its operations—and he or she will agree that communication is the most important function in business. However, it is also the most poorly exercised and most underestimated activity as far as its contribution to and effect on the success or failure of a business entity is. Why is it so important to communicate? Because positive communication performs three vital functions:

- It unites people.
- It spreads knowledge.
- It leaves no room for assumptions and secrecy.

As I mentioned earlier, communication can be achieved in many ways, written and verbal, in person or not, with and without words. With the information age in full swing, our ability to communicate has expanded and new methods have sprung up to enable real-time and seamless exchange of and access to information. In businesses today, we can communicate over wired and wireless devices, the Internet and intranet, in addition to using the traditional means such as meetings, social gathering, newspapers, magazines, letters, and the telephone. Therefore, there should be no excuse for not communicating. However, communicating for the sake of communicating is not good enough. For a meaningful and successful communication, these components must be present:

1. Accurate information.

2. Timely communication.

3. Informative, new information, no repetition.

4. Relevant content.

If any one of all four factors is missing, the communication is worthless. Yes, the "way-to" and the "how-to" communicate are also important, but if the information is wrong, false, inaccurate, too early or too late, the benefits are nullified.

Many have experienced the silent treatment by family members, friend, colleagues, superiors, and customers. Silence is another form of communication, the nonverbal style of communication. Sometimes nonverbal communication is the best. While silence does not address the first item above, the effectiveness of this method of communication is realized through the timing of the silence. It can have much more impact and produce far greater results than if words were used. Nonverbal communication contains strong feelings and emotions that, when used at the right time and in the right situation, can be much more effective than using words.

Even though all forms of communication are valuable and desirable, the one format and method for communicating, which I believe is crucial for a business entity, is meetings. I say this because meetings can, will, and should bring out the facts about various business topics and issues the business entity is or could be facing. They also make visible the human factor, the interaction and exchange that are so crucial in business. It is the reason why face-to-face meetings are still the most popular and practiced in business, especially for high-level executives even though travel, phones, the Internet, and video conferencing are all easily available.

Every department within a business entity holds several meetings during a business day, covering all types of issues and activities such as business, technical, human resources, customer, product, marketing, sales, accounting, finance, and many more. The key to success, however, is not only to have a meeting, but also to have the right meeting at the right time with the right agenda and the right people in attendance.

So many individuals can call meetings, some of which are completely over-lapping, that it is impossible to attend all of them and have the time to perform the daily duties one is responsible for. For certain management levels and during certain periods of the quarter or the year, the number and length of meetings increase considerably, and this is understandable. These periods include forecast-ing, restructuring, developing financial results, preparation for a major customer or account review, end-of-year or end-of-quarter reports, company or product launches, trade show events, and so forth.

In general, however, careful thinking and planning must precede calling a meeting. I have worked in companies where employees, non-managers, individ-ual contributors, regularly spent more than 60 percent of the workweek in meet-ings. That is three full business days each week spent in meetings.

We don't always realize this, but the company and its employees incur a lot of cost when meetings are called without sufficient thought and planning or when they are unnecessary. The costs of meetings include the following:

- Financial cost. Time costs money and so do materials needed for the meet-ings, such as presentations.

- Opportunity loss. Attendees of these meetings could be performing other tasks that have bigger impact on the business. Productivity and effective-ness decline as more time is spent in unnecessary meetings.

- Employee fatigue. Attendees of meetings have to stay late at work or come to work on weekends to finish their daily tasks. Tasks that are considered in evaluating their performance toward achieving the goals for which they were hired. These meetings take away time that otherwise would have been spent on a number of tasks such as finishing a project, learning, and the like.

- Negative impact on the employees' personal life. When employees do not have enough time to complete their assigned daily tasks due to excessive time spent in unnecessary meetings, time is taken away from the employ-ees' personal time—which should be family time, leisure and relaxation—just so they can complete their daily tasks.

- Ill feelings. Frustration, resentment, anger, disrespect, and other strong feelings can arise when employees feel that many meetings are not neces-sary or that the right people are not there. Sometimes these feelings are justified; however, they can create friction within organizations that can escalate and turn into conflicts. In some cases, the real motives for having a meeting is uncovered, thus creating a whole set of other problems for management and the company.

Therefore, it is paramount that the individual calling the meeting first give significant thought to the reasons for the meeting and plan accordingly:

- Identify the issues or topics to be addressed.
- Define the desired results to come out of the meeting.
- Generate and distribute a written request and agenda. Request feedback or input from the chosen attendees regarding the agenda and topics prior to the meeting.
- Set the exact time and place for the meeting. Stay on time.
- Before the meeting, request from the attendees that they prepare or bring whatever information or material needed to address the issues in order to have a productive meeting.
- Determine who should attend the meeting, keeping in mind the total number of attendees. This is crucial for the success of the meeting for several reasons:
  - o If too many people are present, too much time will be needed to conduct and complete the meeting since all attendees must be given a chance to give their points of view in addressing the issues, however briefly.
  - o Too many attendees will also lead to dilution of the inputs since there will be too many of them.
  - o Too many inputs will also cause confusion as to which decision or course of action to follow, and more time will be spent on choosing the right one. Choosing one person's idea over another's can even become a personal issue in a large group.
  - o On the other hand, if there are too few attendees, the ideas and feedback that could be analyzed will be limited in scope.
  - o If the wrong people attend, the meeting will not bear the results desired and could even be a total failure and lead to more problems and difficulties. In other words, the effect will be counterproductive.

At the start of the meeting, the person who called the meeting must do the following:

- Determine whether all the necessary personnel are present. If not, then it may be advantageous for everyone to accept postponing the meeting or to remove the topics that required the presence of those who are not in attendance. This not only preserves the time for the present attendees, but also ensures that the purpose of the meeting or the importance of the particular topic is protected from being overlooked or having insufficient attention paid to it.
- Restate the agenda and ask for any final comments before moving forward with the meeting.
- Identify the persons who will have defined roles, such as the scribe.
- Set the rules for the meeting, the meeting etiquette. This includes which topic to start with, the allotted time for each item, and how to conduct oneself. One of the most important rules to be followed in any meeting is that individuals must address and attack the issue and not the person. Meetings must not be made a place where personal agendas are pursued.
- State the desired outcome of the meeting.
- Identify what the deliverables will be.
- Identify who will deliver what and by when.

Immediately after the meeting a meeting summary must be sent out to all attendees and other stakeholders in the subject.

Figure 8 shows the time spent in meetings by individuals, at various levels of the organization. The shaded area in Figure 8 shows the percentage of the time spent in meetings, which contributes to higher productivity achieved by individuals in those positions, such as individual contributor, managers, or executives. Executives spend the most time in meetings—60 to 70 percent of their time. Next are the mid-level managers, who would appropriately spend approximately 30 to 45 percent of their time in meetings. The least amount of time spent in meetings, 15 to 25 percent, is by individual contributors.

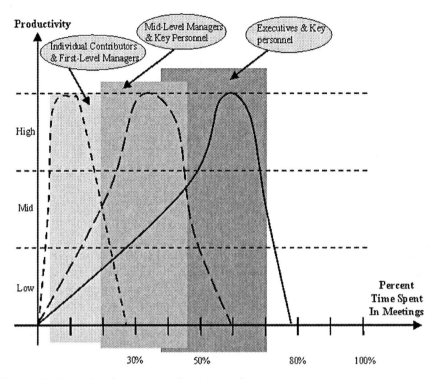

Figure 8 Relationship between productivity and meetings

This is appropriate since they have to execute the plans and decisions made by the company's management teams. The time spent in meetings is also dependent on the company size, the industry it's in, and which stage of existence the company is in: startup, growth, or expansion. Figure 8 also shows that meetings do contribute to productivity and when those individuals at different levels do not attend enough meetings, their productivity and effectiveness decreases.

Sometimes meetings are a waste of time because they are not prepared and conducted properly. Have you ever heard or made comments such as, "We have so many meetings!" "We can't get anything done because we spend so much time in meetings!" "Nothing was accomplished in this meeting because we did not have all the information!" and so on. Most of us have heard these statements and have made some of them as well.

Experience and the appreciation for the exchange of information taught me that effective meetings are a must. However, one must have time to act on the action items and information presented during meetings, as well as demonstrate the ability to perform the tasks he or she is responsible for.

Factors that cause organizations to have too many meetings are as follows:

- Inexperience.
- Confusion, lack of coordination, and direction.
- Indecision.
- Too many problems.
- Micromanaged organization; control syndrome.
- Lack of trust in the organization, in its abilities and personnel.
- Paralyzed organization due to excessive analysis.

These deficiencies give meetings in general a bad reputation. Because of them, in many instances the value and importance of meetings are so undermined and underestimated that insufficient care is given to meeting preparation, organization, and implementation. For the amount of time spent in meetings, one would think that more care and attention would be given to conducting meetings and that companies would demand that. Think of all the meetings, internal and external, that go on during a single business day. Internal meetings such as company meetings, weekly or staff meetings, product development or status meetings, operations meetings, sales meetings, quarterly review meetings, financial meetings, investor meetings, training, and so on. External meetings include customers' meetings, trade shows, conferences, seminars, editor and analyst meetings, and so on. Each one of these meetings is an effort to take a step toward success, for the employee and for the entire organization and its constituencies. However, if the meeting is inefficiently conducted, failure will follow.

No one can deny the importance of meetings and the fact that meetings are the best form of communication in business. When communicating, many of the rules that must be followed to conduct productive meetings apply to having effective communication. Thus, the communicator when communicating must ensure that he or she follows these rules:

- Everyone has ample time to communicate his or her point of view, opinion, or information.
- He or she is personally an excellent listener.
- All the information presented is correct, accurate, and true.
- Don't guess about information; state the uncertainty.
- Do not assume that a given piece of information exists or that everyone knows or does not know about it.
- Everyone must understand the information communicated.
- The ramifications of the information to the company, its business, its products, and its employees must be considered.
- The information communicated must be relevant and usable by the recipients.

Communicating with each other should be one of the first rules to be established by a business entity. Communications must take place up and down the organization's hierarchy and across each level of the hierarchy.

In addition to internal communication, businesses must communicate externally, with their customers, partners, suppliers, shareholders, and investors. Recognizing this need, companies hire and contract public relations (PR) personnel and companies, investor relations (IR) personnel and companies, and place much value on creating excellent marketing and sales organizations. These entities act as a two-ended funnel where one end of the funnel is open to the internals of the company, gathering all relevant information about the company, its business and its products, while the other end of the funnel is open to the outside world spreading that information. Through these organizations—PR, IR, Marketing and Sales—this information is prepared in an agreed-upon format and at the right level of detail before it is communicated externally. Figure 9 illustrates this concept. These organizations, in turn, become the mouth, eyes, and ears for the company, gathering and delivering information from the outside world about market conditions or competitors to the internals of the company. Again, as with other aspects of business, the process is a bidirectional one and is vital to every company.

Figure 9 Communications groups and processes for Public Relations, Investor Relations, Marketing, and Sales

At the end of the day, companies spend a great deal of time, effort, and capital on communications to achieve many goals:

- Informing.
- Educating.
- Protecting all constituents.
- Attracting new ideas.
- Attracting new solutions.
- Avoiding pitfalls and surprises.
- Attracting good employees.
- Being visible.
- Keeping all appropriate and relevant items out in the open for existing and potential constituents.
- Ensuring that all sections of the company are on the same page relating to one another.

Most importantly, communication gives a company that human touch, the human element; it activates the human factors.

Business Collateral

Do Not Make the Value of What You Write Equal
Only to That of the Paper It Is Written On

Another important method for communicating is through written documents. Documents, collateral material used by business entities for internal and external purposes, contain information that validates every aspect of the business entity and all that it stands for. There are three categories of business collateral:

1. To establish the business—legal documents, business name, type of business, and so on.

2. To conduct the business—business plans, product specifications, user's manuals, customer presentations, financial documents, and so forth.

3. To define what the company stands for and how to run its business—policies and procedures.

The collateral material that makes up each of these categories must be carefully created. From applying for the business name to the most complex procedures, careful thought must be given to the matter. The quality of the collateral material used by a company is not only a reflection of the business itself but also a representation of the individuals who create it. The quality of the collateral is an indication of the individuals' character, including these aspects:

- Ethics and etiquette.
- Quality as people and professionals and their self-esteem.
- Beliefs and values.
- Mental capacity and intellect.
- Appreciation and understanding of their business.
- Talents, expertise, and experience.

As stated, the contents of each piece of collateral will point to the character of the individuals who created them. It is, therefore, to the benefit of all involved to ensure that what is put into business collateral will portray the accurate and desired image of the company and its personnel to achieve the desired outcome. In other words, "put in what you want to get out."

Out of the three categories of collateral material listed above, only item 2, conducting the business, will be addressed here.

Hundreds of document types make up the total business collateral required to conduct business. Each department has its own list of documents to monitor and measure itself with as well as to share with internal and external organizations that it interacts with. Utmost care must be given to creating the business collateral. These documents drive and lead to decisions that will impact every element of a company and its personnel. As I stated, every company must communicate to its employees the value of documentation and train them to create documents with accurate and relevant content pertinent to their specific function and organization. Factors contributing to inaccuracies in the contents of documents include the following:

- Inadequate experience and expertise.
- Oversight.
- Outdated information.
- Wrong assumptions and judgments.
- Inaccurate or poor decisions; previous and present decisions.

Even though these factors can have serious ramifications for the company, its business and personnel, they can be overcome with the proper training and due diligence. It is very simple to achieve. There are two guidelines to follow when trying to eliminate inaccuracies in documents:

1. When a document is intended for internal use only, obtain feedback from the employees—communicate within.

2. When the document is intended for internal and external use, obtain feedback from the employees and a select set of constituents, two to three at most.

Many of today's documents are missing the personal touch of the individuals who are responsible for preparing them. As these individuals climb the career ladder, they seem to equate that success with the act of relinquishing document preparation responsibilities to their assistants and support personnel. The documents I would like to focus on as examples are memos, letters, and presentations. What seems to happen is that these executives or senior managers scribble some things on a few sheets of paper and hand them to their assistants to create the electronic version (PowerPoint, for example), or they dictate a few sentences to their assistants in an effort to craft the memo, letter, or presentation. This behavior is demonstrated by many executives in many companies and in many industries, regardless of the importance of the presentation or the memo. Yes, there are instances, and certain documents, that justify delegation, but those must not be documents that carry messages or positioning statements about the company or its products. When individuals relegate document preparation to another, they miss the valuable opportunity to do the following:

- Add their personal touch to the content.
- Make corrections, changes, or improvements to their initial draft, changing the content as they enter the information, typing it in on their computers or laptops.

- Go through the process of reviewing the presentation in their own mind while entering the content, allowing themselves to better organize the content to achieve the desired smooth and effective flow.
- Better learn the content.
- Better understand the effectiveness and impact of the memo, letter, or presentation on the target audience.

By giving up the abovementioned benefits, the individual is sacrificing the quality, effectiveness, and strength of what he or she intended to communicate to the target audience. Once sacrificed, the opportunity is forever lost. Yes, there will be other memos and presentations to be written, but the content, purpose, timing, and audience may be different. One would want to have the personal touch, wording sequence, sentence structures, opinions, and feelings to be conveyed to the target audiences.

In a nutshell, the basic requirements to create a company's business collateral are to have an open and well-crafted communication following the proper etiquette in gathering and presenting the information. Don't forget the ethical part, either.

The Wisdom in What I Learned

One's Conduct Is One's Most Accurate Form of Communication

Honest and Open Communication Is a Sign of Confidence

Communication Is Business Music

Be True to Yourself

The Wise Person Is One Who Knows What to Say, When to Say It, Whom to Say It to, How Much to Say, and How to Say It

Do Not Make the Value of What You Write Equal Only to That of the Paper It Is Written On

One Is What One Says, What One Reads, and What One Writes

Communication Enables GUT FEEL

Communication Is Magnetic Energy—It Pulls People Toward A Common Goal

Chapter Six

Organization

Organize with Compassion Using the Mind and Heart

Managing the worldwide marketing and sales organization for Company OK, I was planning to set up two offices in Europe, one in the UK and the other in Germany, to manage the business and support the customers. The regional managers I hired to manage the two offices were very qualified individuals. However, I had to be sensitive to which part of Europe each office was to be responsible for, having knowledge of sensitivities that had existed since World War II. Based on this knowledge, I made the decision to split Europe in a way that was uncommon within the high-tech industry. Many who knew of my plan commented that this was an unusual split and would not work. However, the result was a very smooth and successful organization that established strong business relationships in the region and secured significant agreement with key customers worth millions of dollars for the company. One of the key reasons for the success was the attention paid to the human element and the acknowledgement of the idiosyncrasies and sensitivities of the population in the entire region. The organizational structure must consider such matters very carefully if success is to be attained.

What is an organization? Simply put, it is groups of individuals, each with the responsibility to perform specific functions. These functions can be related to sales, finance, marketing, support, or manufacturing. Different companies have different functional areas and structure. The common building block, however, is the personnel, the people who will make up the body of the organization.

One can take all those high-rise buildings with all the steel, concrete, and glass, their enormous size and beauty and try to create a business entity. It simply will not work. Without exception, all that grandeur cannot and will not create success without the people. People build all these majestic structures, anyway. Again, we come back to the famous phrase, "by the people, for the people."

The fundamental question, though, is this: "For whom and why do businesses organize themselves and set up organizational structures?" The answer is "for the people," for internal and external personnel, for the employees and constituents, for investors and suppliers. These are the purposes of setting up an organizational structure:

- ˙Create structure.
- Become organized.
- Enable success.
- Eliminate confusion.
- Support other organizations within the company.
- Ensure that personnel skills match the functional areas they are assigned to.
- Determine accountability when successful or failing.
- Facilitate measurability to monitor progress.

However, an organization's structure must be set up in accordance with the following:

- The skills of its personnel.
- Its business model and plan.
- Goals and objectives—what it intends to accomplish and when.
- Its products and or services.
- Its target markets and customers.
- Its competitors.

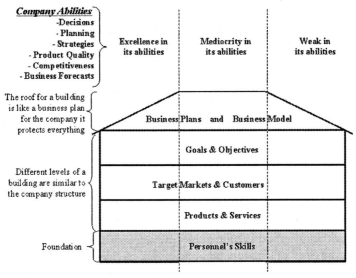

Figure 10 Organizing determines what is available and what is unavailable to a business entity.

Figure 10 shows what the makeup of an organized company looks like. At the foundation are its personnel. It is through its personnel that a company will be able to organize itself and conduct business, set goals, and achieve them. A proper organizational structure will aid the personnel in achieving success. The rising part of the roof on the left side of the building in Figure 10 indicates a company that is growing due to excellence of its decision making, planning competitiveness, and so on. The center section is a flat, mediocre company. The right side, with the declining roof, indicates a company with poor organization skills and capabilities. Remember, organizing does not apply only to the company's structure. It applies to everything from organizing and planning an activity or process to organizing efforts to penetrate a new market or offer a new product.

Organizational Ethics and Etiquette

To Succeed, Create a Living Organization,
Flexible and Open

I was working at Company J for a manager who was extremely bright, with a superb marketing mind and ability. This hotshot marketing director, who was doing an exceptional job for the company as a whole, was beginning to establish a very strong reputation among his peers and superiors, the senior management.

His manager, the vice president of marketing, became threatened by his performance and reputation within the corporate ranks. The vice president, in an effort to protect his position, justified and created a new layer of management between him and this director to weaken the director's influence. Instead of being commended for his achievements and contributions to the company, this director was demoted unfairly and unethically.

In essence, the director was indirectly demoted. This meant that everyone in the director's group was demoted as well. The result was that most members of the director's team, except for one person, left the company. This exodus included the director himself. Eventually the vice president was fired as well. However, the damage to the company was already done and the opportunity cost was enormous.

Organizations are not meant to be self-serving empires. They are intended to augment and coexist with other organizations within the company to make the whole, a strong and functioning body of a business entity. Taking it a step further, a company will have to coexist with other companies within its own industry. Therefore, a clear structure is necessary so that other companies know how to interact with this company. However, in some cases, organizational structure and hierarchical structures are counterproductive. Most of these counterproductive organizational structures create more roadblocks for the individuals operating within them than not. However, some are set to be self-serving with hidden agendas, and those are the most dangerous. Organizational structures should not be set up for these purposes:

- To discredit or render other organizations weak or obsolete.
- To strengthen an organization or person's position over another's within the company.
- To justify the existence of a particular organization or position to justify the employment of one or more individuals.

Additionally, organizational structures must not be limiting and adding rigidity to the operation. Many companies have unintentionally set up organizational structures that are virtually impossible to make efficient and productive. Organizing is good; however, there is a point where a company becomes over organized, and that's when the structure becomes very restricting to creativity and achievement.

On the other hand, some companies set up organizations to accommodate available personnel. Such organizations also cut into efficiency and effectiveness while making it very difficult and confusing to make decisions and progress. It creates another layer of organization other groups will have to go through or deal with to achieve their objectives. Even though the available personnel are good, groups should not be created for that reason. It is best to find a place for them in another organization if the company does not wish to let them go.

Figure 11 shows the relationship between efficiency, flexibility, and organizational structure. As companies effectively organize themselves creating the necessary departments, they become more efficient and their flexibility increases, promoting productivity and achievement. However, as more organizational structure is created, the efficiency and flexibility begins to decrease. This is one of the signs of having an organization with multiple layers, requiring multiple procedures to get anything done.

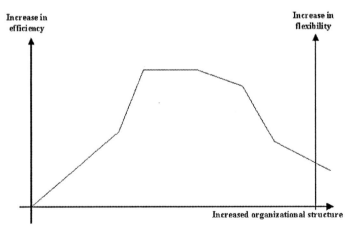

Figure 11 Effects of over organizing

Building a company requires the creation of several organizations. The act of building the company is like completing a jigsaw puzzle. One cannot force a piece of the puzzle into the wrong place. It has to fit smoothly; otherwise, it will create gaps between itself and the other pieces, or break. Each organization must be created at the right time. Each must fit the plan intended for the company and its business, not the other way around. A company must not enter a business or undertake a specific activity just because organizations or personnel are available.

If the belief is, or there is proof that a certain organization is not needed, is inefficient, or has become a burden on another organization, the proper etiquette to resolve the matter is through proposals and open communications. The process with which organizations are created and dismantled must be carefully executed in order to maintain a sound company by protecting the integrity of its personnel. If the change is made in an unethical manner—secretly, manipulatively, and maliciously, without the proper etiquette—the outcome will have an adverse effect on the personnel and the business. Even if the change is done ethically, but clumsily, without proper planning, the effect will also be negative.

Two questions must be answered before any decision is made to alter the organizational structure of a company:

1. How will the change impact the company's ability to conduct business effectively?

2. How will changing the organizational structure affect the employees of the entire company?

The correct decision will be fruitful and effective and will lead to successes for all concerned. On the other hand, a wrong or premature decision regarding the process and the method of making the change will disable the entire company and cause confusion and failure. Uncorrected, this will eventually lead to the demise of the business entity.

So many companies in many industries make so many organizational changes that it becomes confusing to the employees and all constituents. They grapple to understand and follow the reasoning behind the changes. Companies hire and lay off employees so frequently that loyalty is nonexistent. In addition, positions are created, even at the senior management levels strictly to push ineffective senior managers into those positions so they are removed from the day-to-day operation and decision-making process and their influence is curbed. This is not only costly, demoralizing, and demeaning, but is also unfair and unethical.

We have all worked for companies that had layoffs, and some of us have experienced being laid off. It does not feel good, especially when people you have worked with for many years lose their jobs; their livelihood is put in danger and jeopardy. The effects layoffs have on personnel's careers and families are tremendous. Companies go on a hiring spree one year, creating new organizations or enlarging existing ones, then turn around and lay off as many employees as they hired, plus more, the following year. I always wondered why that is. A company should never have to hire and lay off its employees or change organizational structure, once every year or two. Companies attribute their hiring and layoff activities to several reasons, including the following:

- Downturn of the economy.
- The loss or decline of revenue.
- Lack of new customer commitments to purchase products.
- Changing their business model.
- Exiting some of their markets or geographies.
- Discontinuing some of their products and services.

Some of the above is valid and does happen. However, the reality is that companies that go through layoffs and organizational changes every couple of years do so for reasons such as these:

- Bad decisions that were made previously.
- Poor planning.
- Poor strategies.
- Poor or wrong product selection.
- Poor product quality and/or performance.
- Poor competitiveness, strategies, and tactics.
- Poor forecast of their business potential.
- Wrong target market.
- Presence in the wrong region.

It is understandable and acceptable for companies to change their organizational structure and, therefore, have a reduction in work force for such reasons as these:

- A business is no longer viable.
- A business downturn occurred due to events not under their control.
- The company or its headquarters were moved to a new region.
- The company exited a region or market segment.

However, these events are neither common nor frequent. If companies plan properly, they will not have frequent layoffs. For example, if a company is not securing enough new customers to maintain its profitability, it may either have layoffs or reorganize itself. However, a closer look will reveal that the real reason is that the wrong products or features were implemented, poor competitive strategies were pursued or the market was not ready yet for such products. In any event any company's success goes back to good planning, execution, and sound decision-making. The company's management should know how to do all three.

Proper planning must be created and followed to determine the type and size of organization that will be needed to get the job done. If too large of an organization is created, it is possible that not all employees will have enough relevant work to do. In such a case, investors' dollars are wasted. Many companies grow prematurely and too quickly. When this happens, excuses will be given to justify the creation, even existence, of certain positions. The company will begin to grow abnormally, and the organization will look like patchwork. Three questions must be answered when creating an organization or a new position:

1. What are its roles?
2. Where will it fit in the company?
3. How will it help the rest of the company achieve its goals?

Justification is realized when these questions are clearly answered. On the other hand, the following questions should be answered when eliminating an organization or position:

1. What will the effects of the change be on remaining personnel?
2. What are the roles and responsibilities being eliminated?
3. Are these roles and responsibilities still needed?
4. How will the needed roles be performed after the elimination?
5. If the roles are not needed, why were they originally created?
6. What, when, and how should the change be communicated to the rest of the company?

An organizational structure for a company is like the map of a country. One has to follow the map to maneuver his or her way over the terrain to reach the desired destination. It is the map used by the employees, management, customers, vendors, investors, and partners to achieve the desired result, which, at the end of the day, is to produce products, offer services, generate revenue, and create prosperity. So, if one wants to purchase a product, sales gets the call. If one needs to learn the status of a product under development, marketing gets the call. If there is a problem with a product already purchased, customer service or support is called. For financial information, the accounting or finance department is contacted and so on. All these departments are connected through processes, procedures, and personnel, creating the whole of the company. If any of the pieces of the whole are weak, the entire company is weakened, eventually leading the entire organizational structure to weaken and possibly collapse.

Years ago, I interviewed at a startup company. The position was a vice president of marketing. The product area and target markets were in line with what I was looking for. The company's first product was in development and sample availability was eighteen months away.

All this was fine until I began asking about the current organization and future growth plans. What I heard was a formula for disaster. The company was currently seeking to hire not only a vice president of marketing but also a vice president of sales and a vice president of business development, all to be hired within the next six months. My next question was "How will the roles and responsibilities of all these senior individuals be defined?" It was important to understand how all three were to function without tripping over each other, causing confusion within the company as well as within the company's targeted customer base. Not only was this prospect dangerous to the company's existence, but also in the end it could negatively reflect on the three vice presidents' performance and reputation within the company and within the industry as a whole. I did not pursue the opportunity, and the company is no longer in business.

How to Organize

Don't Organize in a Void! Do It with People in Mind

I was working for Company S, headquartered in Europe. They had decided to establish an operation in the United States based in the Silicon Valley. I was hired as the vice president and general manager and was chartered to set up the operation, manage the budget, and recruit the heads of the different functional areas, such as marketing, sales, engineering, manufacturing, finance.

As outlined in the original organizational chart, all the functional heads were to report to the chief executive officer of the company, who was based in Europe. As a general manager based in the United States, I found it very difficult to manage the organization when the senior managers did not report to me. Even though I was responsible for making sure the operation was running smoothly and efficiently, I had no say into their day-to-day activities and deliverables.

When I proposed a change to the organization and the reporting structure, the chief executive officer declined to accept stating that he wanted everyone, including me to report to him. Since I was not interested in an administrative role at that time of my career, I decided to resign. Six months later, the company closed its U.S. operations, partly due to an economic downturn. A year after that, it went out of business. Wrong organizational structure, process, reporting structure, and wrong management decisions were the causes of the failure. More than eighty employees were adversely affected, and a promising technology and over $70M in raised capital was lost.

As I mentioned earlier, an organizational structure is needed to enable employees to succeed and to eliminate internal and external confusion. The examples used here are relevant and applicable to all types of companies; however, the details relate to companies in the high-tech industry.

When setting up the organization for a company, three issues must be addressed when planning the organization's structure:

1. What type of organizational structure to start with.

2. When to expand the organization.

3. What to expand the organization to.

Each of the three items listed above need to be addressed with the next one in mind and in the order listed. The type of organization to be established initially must be carefully thought through and implemented to make later expansion smooth and possible. However, the structure of the foundation—and the foundation is the starting organizational structure—must be sound. The soundness will depend on the health and quality of the personnel and the combination of a sound foundation and quality personnel will be the critical formula to the success of the business entity.

Setting up an organizational structure is relatively simple and should not be complicated. It involves having and applying common sense, utilizing personal and professional experiences. When trying to determine an organizational structure, stop and think first. In your mind's eye go through and identify the business processes and activities that will have to take place to achieve the desired goals for which the organization is being set up. Envision what each process will entail to grow the business and the organization. Go through the thought and analytical process to determine the answers to the following five questions when trying to establish the right organization:

1. What phase of its existence is the company in?

2. Does the company have the right management team?

3. What does the company offer? Products or services?

4. Are the products or services developed and available?

5. Does the company have the right skilled personnel?

The answers to the above questions should help start the process of setting up the organization. However, the starting point will hinge on whether this is a reevaluation or correction of existing organizations.

Reevaluating Existing Organizational Structure

In an established company, there are three reasons for the organizational structure to be reevaluated:

1. To meet the requirements of a new business plan or strategy for penetrating a new market, entering a new region, producing new products, or a combination of the three.

2. To correct the existing organizational structure in a turnaround effort of the company's business or improve its profitability. Part of a turnaround effort also includes exiting a product, market, or region.

3. To make better use of the expertise and skill set of the company's existing employees.

When reevaluating the organizational structure, the issue that must be addressed first is item number 1 above. This is key because the effort to execute item 1 will influence every decision and touch every department in an organization. The following factors should be considered when reevaluating an organizational structure:

- Does the company have the right skill sets and experience to set up an organizational structure to develop the new product, penetrate the new market or region?

- Does the organization have the right management team and management structure?

- Can the organization handle the new growth?

- What are the characteristics of the new region or market? Are there specific habits, customs, life styles, economic or political situations, and so on to consider?

- Is the product sufficiently viable in the long run to justify the existence of the organization to develop it?

- Is this the right time for this undertaking?
- Can the new organizational structure meet the company's financial guidelines?
- Can the organizational structure make the company competitive?

If the answer is "no" to any one of these questions, the company must determine whether it can change the situation. This can be done by acquiring the right skill sets in time, or changing the competitiveness of the company, and so on. If the answer is still no, nothing should be done. If the answer is yes to all of the above questions, or it can change any of the conditions, then company can begin the data-gathering process to put the plans and action items in place to optimize the organizational structure. The data-gathering process must include answers to the following questions:

- Does the company have enough financial and other resources to successfully undertake the efforts of penetrating a new market, entering a new region, or developing a new product?
- Who are the competitors that the company must pay attention to and can the company successfully compete against them?
- Are there enough mature customers? Who are the customers that must be won, and which competitors' products do these customers currently use?
- Are there business and product plans that outline the timeline for identifying success factors, the measurability and accountability of the progress, and its results?
- Can the company sustain itself after penetrating the new market, new region, or producing the new product? Does the company have sufficient financial and other resources to sustain the new business and activities? This is a crucial question for the company and, if not addressed early on, it could kill the company by putting an enormous burden on other internal organizations that might not be ready to handle the extra activity load. The company must be able to grow in the new market and geography and must be able to produce next generation products to the first one. As business grows so do the organization's needs for more personnel, more equipment, more expertise, larger facilities, and so on, and the company must be ready, willing, and able to oblige.

When expanding a business into new regions where new human factors will come into existence and must be learned, understood, and respected, serious care and attention must be given to the implementation. The human factors in the new region are the outcome of issues like these:

- The way people live and interact socially and professionally.
- Cultural diversity, customs and habits.
- Educational level of the population.
- Historical issues.
- Political climate.
- Religions represented.
- Economic situation such as the relative size of upper, middle, and lower classes.

Correcting an Organizational Structure

To correct a broken organization, the same questions must be asked, and the same analysis conducted. However, now the organizational structure must relate to the company's existing products, markets, and regions. Justification must be given for continuing or halting the efforts and presence in the existing markets, or regions or producing the current products. In a broken organization or in a turnaround effort, management and all personnel must review and analyze the situation in an effort to identify the reasons that caused the company to fail and reach its current state. This involves going over every aspect of the organization.

It is for this reason that the way to organize a business entity must be carefully thought out and planned, taking into consideration the human element of business.

The Four Phases of a Company's Life Cycle

Just as every person goes through various phases while growing up, so does every business entity and its internal organizational structure. The needs of the business and personnel will cause the organization to respond and become fluid and dynamic.

"Don't bite off more than you can chew" are words to live by when setting up an organization. In the beginning, an organization must be simple, agile, and quick. When setting up an organization, careful attention must be given to where the company is in its life cycle in order to better determine what the new organizational structure should be. For any business entity, there will be four major phases that it will pass through during the course of its existence:

Phase 1:   Startup
Phase 2:   Growth

Phase 3:   Expansion
Phase 4:   Exit

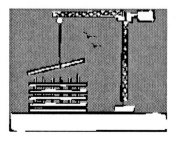

Phase 1: Startup

In a startup company, the product or service is not yet available and is only an idea; the organizational issues are different and simpler than those for established companies. However, the organizational issues for a startup are more crucial for its long-term survival, and management must make sure that organizational structure is done right from the outset.

All startup companies are created with a group of people getting together to brainstorm a product idea in an effort to bring the product idea to fruition. The first task for the individual, or individuals, with the product idea is to recruit the right team to further develop the product idea, ensuring along the way that the personalities and characteristics of the different individuals match and complement each other's.

Remember that one of the most important realizations for any business entity is to recognize which skills are missing and which are present. These include functional skills such as engineering, marketing, and sales, and interpersonal skills needed.

- In this phase, the founders and early employees of the company must validate the plans and the early decisions made and confirm the direction of the company as to its products or services, target markets, and regions to sell to and compete in. These are some of the questions that must be answered by management in the startup phase:

- What is the company's product or service?

- How and where should the company compete? This will address the target market segment and region.

- What type of organization should be created? This will address the types and size of the various functional areas.

During this phase, the company must have focus and commitment. Only one major product must be developed and introduced. One or two more "derivative" products can be produced. These derivatives can be very similar to the first major product with minor enhancements or feature additions.

Similarly, the company must focus on a single market segment. Multiple markets can be the kiss of death for a startup company because different market segments have different requirements and characteristics that will require special attention, organization, products, and support. This would be a daunting task and difficult to achieve even for established companies let alone a startup. With a single major product for a single market segment, the number of employees needed would also be contained. Typically, fewer than 50 employees will suffice; however, some market segments and products may have additional requirements that would justify additional personnel.

The startup company should first install the following functional areas:

- The portion of the executive team that includes the CEO, CFO, Chief Technical Officer (CTO), and head of marketing or business development with marketing know-how.

- Engineering to develop the product.

- Marketing to develop relationships with target customers and validate the product's features and the chosen market.

- Finance/accounting to manage the company's finances.

- Experienced professionals with no significant requirements for training because the company has no time or bandwidth to train new hires and bring them up to speed. Everyone must carry his or her load and hit the ground running.

The functional areas—marketing, engineering, sales, and so forth—in a startup phase must be created in stages as milestones are reached. The stages and processes for a company that offers products vs. services are also different. Here I will address the stages and processes for a startup company that offers products.

Stage One

- Ensure that the head of product development is on board when the company begins operations. If none of the founders are qualified to take up the role, then that position must be filled first because, in a startup, this person must be hands-on and able to actually develop the product. The head of development will then hire the needed personnel to develop the product. Building the engineering and support groups will be ongoing during each of the six stages. During the first stage, however, the founders will continuously be searching for capital, validating their business plan, and putting the organizational structure in place.

Stage Two

- Establish the finance and marketing or business development organizations. The headcount for each of these departments should be low. The finance individual will work on raising capital for the operation and will maintain the accounting books. The marketing/business development individual will work on validating the product features and specifications, developing the product collateral material, conducting market and competitive analyses, and begin developing customer relationships. The company will continuously monitor and validate its earlier decisions and strategies and create the company's policies and procedures.

Stage Three

- Expand the finance and marketing organizations.

Stage Four

- Hire the head of the sales organization. Continue to expand all departments as business dictates.

Stage Five

- Expand the sales and customer support organizations. Keep them small at this stage. Grow the company as business justifies.

Stage Six

- Hire the head of operations. This person will oversee the day-to-day operations of the company. This is a key role if manufacturing is involved. Manufacturing activities, however, could be internal or external: either the company does the manufacturing itself or contracts it out to a manufacturing company. In either case, there should be a person who will oversee the manufacturing activities. If manufacturing is involved, outsourcing it is the way to go and the head of operations will monitor this activity as well.

Phase 2: Growth

In this phase, the company has to reevaluate its offerings and decisions made in the startup phase of its existence. In addition, the company has to determine its growth strategies and directions in its chosen market and chosen regions. It must evaluate organizational issues and identify any additional new products, markets, and regions to consider participating in. Here are some of the questions management must answer in the growth phase:

- Are the company's products or services still the right ones?
- Are the company's target market and region still viable?
- Is the company's organization still appropriate to address the target market's and regions' requirements?
- How, where, and when should the company grow? This question relates to the size of the company and its product offering, target markets, and regions. In other words, does it have enough resources to grow?

At this point, the company should still maintain its focus and try to excel in its product offering, target market, and region. Therefore, no more than two major products should be pursued with two derivatives at most for each major product. The target markets should remain contained to ensure superior offering and support. In doing so, the company's growth will also have to be controlled to ensure efficiency and accountability.

The company must install and expand the following functional areas in the growth phase:

- Those that were created during the company's startup phase.
- The sales department.
- The customer support organization.
- The Information Technology (IT) department.
- Relevant areas of the company driven by its business and revenue, product, market, and constituents' needs.

Phase 3: Expansion

In this phase the company is basically committed to the strategies crafted for its current product offerings, markets, and regions and is seeking to expand its business into new markets and regions, with new products and/or acquisition. Here are some of the questions management must answer in the expansion phase:

- Should the company expand? If so, how should it expand and how much should it expand? This will address expanding organically or through mergers and acquisitions.

- Are the company's existing products and services still viable? What other products should be offered? Should these products be developed in-house or acquired? If acquired, should they be purchased or licensed?

- Are the company's target markets and regions still viable? What new market and/or regions should be considered?

- Is the company's organization appropriate to address the requirements of its current market segments and regions? Is it appropriate for a new product, market segment, and region?

If the company is in financial trouble at this phase, it must review its business plan and operation. This must be done at all phases, especially if the company has been in existence for few years and should have more financial stability than in earlier phases.

If, on the other hand, the company is in good financial standing, it should investigate expansion possibilities. A company should always seek to expand its product offering. However, it should carefully weigh expanding into new markets and regions because, as I mentioned earlier, expanding into a new market or region is a much more complex and demanding undertaking. Just because a product or service offering is expanded does not mean the company must expand into new markets and regions. The company can do so within its existing market.

A company must take the following actions when considering expansion:

- Expand every department in accordance with its business requirements and demands.

- Acquire personnel who will evaluate expansion opportunities, set directions, and monitor the expansion after the fact.

- Select staff in accordance with the requirements of the new products, markets, and/or regions. This could mean establishing a sales office in a new country, hiring specific product experts, or launching a promotional campaign for a new market.

Phase 4: Exit

An exit strategy is an important phase that must be considered and made available when certain conditions or situations present themselves to the company. There are various ways for companies to exit their business, product, market, or region:

- Shut down. Lay off all employees and liquidate all assets. This of course is the least desirable option.

- Merge with another company in the same industry or in a vertical industry.
- Get acquired by a company from within its industry or by a company in a vertical industry.
- Go public through an Initial Public Offering (IPO). This of course, is for a startup only.

During this phase, the company must control its expenses and maintain a nimble and lean organization, with respect to size. This is necessary in case the company wants to be acquired, in which case it should show low expenditure.

In each of the four phases, there must be close scrutiny as to the number of employees, especially at the executive levels, and the types of organizations, departments, and groups to install to support the company's plans and businesses.

Figure 12 summarizes only the startup, growth, and expansion phases of a company's life cycle and the structure needed to conduct an efficient and successful business. At the beginning of each phase, management must ask questions that will provide the answers as to the condition of the company, its growth path and overall health. Some of these questions are listed in the stepped boxes above the timeline arrow in the figure. The questions are influenced by the company's place in its life cycle and will vary for each phase.

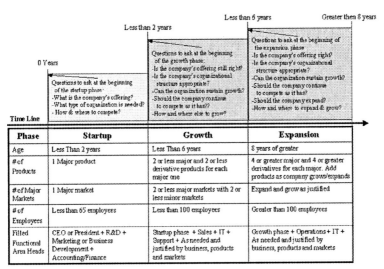

Phase	Startup	Growth	Expansion
Age	Less Than 2 years	Less Than 6 years	8 years of greater
# of Products	1 Major product	2 or less major and 2 or less derivative products for each major one	4 or greater major and 4 or greater derivatives for each major. Add products as company grows/expands
# of Major Markets	1 Major market	2 or less major markets with 2 or less minor markets	Expand and grow as justified
# of Employees	Less than 65 employees	Less than 100 employees	Greater than 100 employees
Filled Functional Area Heads	CEO or President + R&D + Marketing or Business Development + Accounting/Finance	Startup phase + Sales + IT + Support + As needed and justified by business, products and markets	Growth phase + Operations + IT + As needed and justified by business, products and markets

Figure 12 Phased organizational structures

Establishing an organizational structure is a process that has a time factor. Do things in stages, one step at a time, at the right time. Establish organizations as they become needed and can contribute to the business. Organizations must not be idle while costing the company financially and demoralizing the personnel who don't feel they are contributing or being respected by other departments. Do not grow organizations to satisfy egos. Grow them as the business justifies. When an organization's size is not justified, the effects will ripple through the entire company causing disharmony, difficulty in managing, resentment, and low personnel morale, among other things. These problems will cause the organization to lose focus on the tasks at hand. This objective will not be met without taking care of the employees, making sure they are a team assigned to meaningful tasks and challenges.

Remember the startup company I interviewed with that was planning to hire a vice president of marketing, a vice president of sales, and a vice president of business development all at the same time when the product was still eighteen months away from introduction. Large organizations bring about large requirements, large responsibilities, and larger headaches if not implemented properly. If the company is not mature enough yet to handle the size and complexity that comes with large organizations, a quick expansion could be detrimental to the company's survival. The key reason for this is that the needs of the organization will not match the abilities of its employees, thus causing them to fail or perform below average and eventually get into a downward spiral that will lead to the demise of the company.

The Wisdom in What I Learned

Organize with Compassion Using the Mind and Heart

To Succeed, Create a Living Organization, Flexible and Open

Don't Organize in a Void! Do It with People in Mind

Chapter Seven

Policies and Procedures

Policies, Like Ethics, Define the Right Things to Do
Procedures, Like Etiquette, Outline the Right Way of Doing Them

The CEO of Company LOG was searching for a vice president of marketing. The company was in existence for several years but was still operating as a startup. I met with the CEO and had a good interview. However, my concern was about the financial health of the company. So, I asked the CEO how much money the company had and how long would the company survive with that amount. The CEO said that they had enough money to last them six to nine months, during which time their new products would be out and generating significant revenue. I was comfortable with that and was up to the task of making sure we do introduce the new products on time to generate revenue. When I was three months into the job, the CEO called his staff to a meeting and informed us that the company was tight on capital and that it is possible that we wouldn't get paid the following month. I was shocked. How could this happen so suddenly when only three months ago I was told we had enough money to last us six to nine months? I asked the CEO this during the meeting. He did not like it. A week later he called me to his office and said, "You told us you had an MBA from Notre Dame." I said, "Yes, College of Notre Dame." He blushed and said "Not the University of Notre Dame?" He then looked at my resume and confirmed that he had made a mistake. The damage was already done for he had gone ahead and called the University of Notre Dame to inquire if I had attended there. The trust was shattered and we parted ways immediately.

The policies and procedures of a company define what type of a company it is. The values, beliefs, and ethical standards of every employee go into the makeup, creation, and execution of the company's policies. Ethical people create ethical policies while ethical policies support and guide people and keep everyone honest. The above story presents a situation which would make one wonder what type of policies and procedures such a misleading CEO would create and support.

For any business entity to be successful, its policies and procedures must influence and mold every element of its organization, its processes, and its activities including: recruiting; compensation; termination; product development and approval procedures; business plan preparation and approval; execution and implementation of various activities; accounting practices; marketing activities; sales processes; employee benefits; performance reviews; customer support; vendor selection, and so on. However, some companies put more emphasis on their policies and procedures than others do in that there is more fairness, consistency, and care in creating them and a stronger commitment to implementing them.

Many companies display their policies in the lobbies of their company buildings. They do so because these policies define who the company is and what are the laws by which the company, through its personnel, conducts itself. Sound policies and procedures are a testament to the importance of establishing trust with the company's constituencies through ethical policies and sound procedures. Everyone who works with and for the company must have this trust to create success. When trusting a company, one trusts the people running the company. When the employees conduct themselves and their business in accordance with ethical policies and procedures, constituencies will trust every offering of the company. They may not like the offering itself, but at least they know what they have at hand.

Sadly, many of these policies, once created, are hung on walls in lobbies, conference rooms, and offices never to be read, acknowledged or even noticed again, and their content and meaning is forgotten, overlooked, or ignored. Eventually, undermined policies will be noticed and at this point the issue of reevaluating these policies and procedures must be raised. It is possible that the old policies and procedures have weakened, in which case changes and modifications must be made. However, if it is determined that the existing policies and procedures are still strong, valid, and desirable, then the effort to communicate and reinforce their meaning must be undertaken by managements in a formal and organized setting.

Every company has many policies and procedures that help it conduct its business. However, the two I will discuss here pertain to money and compensation, and recruiting and retention. I chose these two because they have powerful impact on the personnel and the company.

Ethics in Crafting Policies and Procedures

Policies and Procedures Protect People and Business

Companies make an enormous effort to present and display ethical business practices. They create ethics committees, senior level ethics management position, ethics memoranda, and so forth. Instead, those companies should revisit their existing list of policies and procedures and reiterate them, bring them back to life, and more importantly, manage according to these policies and procedures.

All employees must know and clearly understand their company's policies and procedures. I don't mean a word-for-word memorization, but every line item or concept must be remembered and understood. We have all heard statements like "walk the talk" or "manage by example" and so on. These are all correct and wonderful phrases to apply, but they must be in line with the company's policies and procedures in order to materialize into success.

I mentioned earlier that policies outline the right things to do and these are outcomes of being honest, fair, compassionate, and receptive.

When the policies are in place, the procedures to carry out these policies must be crafted and followed throughout the company. Again, policies outline the right things to do. Procedures outline the right way of implementing the policies. These procedures are the step-by-step descriptions and implementation of the company's policies. One may ask, "What is the difference between the procedure to approve a business plan and that for a product development?" The answer is that there should be no difference in the intent, but the personnel and tactics will be different. The intent should be to conduct the process ethically and with the good of the employees and the company in mind.

As I mentioned in this chapter's opening remarks, policies and procedures are created from the values, beliefs, and ethical standards of every employee. Therefore, when approving a business plan or product development plan for example, employees involved must not follow "the end justifies the means" mentality. The means must be ethical and the end must be "success and retained integrity."

It is not acceptable to live by the phrase "the end justifies the means" unless the means are guided. Otherwise this is a recipe for chaos and disaster. Employees will then find justification for their actions, justification for the means they pursued to reach an end, successful or otherwise. In business, the end does not and must not justify the means! When the means are unethical, the result will be a company that looks like a house of cards that will crumple under the slightest of pressures.

Think of all the companies, such as WorldCom, Tyco, and Enron that were caught between the years 2000 and 2003 with fraudulent accounting practices that presented those companies as profitable and successful. I am sure the policies and procedures of these companies were of the highest ethical standards, founded on the premise of improving the well-being and the quality of living for millions of people. Unfortunately, these policies and procedures were not followed. Here, the practice of "the end justifies the means" was in big play, but in the wrong way. Investors and employees were tricked into thinking the companies' stock values were accurately depicting the state of the companies' current and future business potential. The investors and employees invested heavily. Investors put in billions of dollars to finance the growth of these companies, not knowing that they were financing the life styles of the executives who were running them. In the meantime, the employees of these companies risked and lost their entire retirement plans and financial savings by investing in those companies' stocks based on the false promises made by company executives.

I have also worked for companies that pursued the "end justifies the means" method of achieving their objectives. However, remember it is the individuals running these companies, their executives, CEOs, and managers, who are making these decisions. Therefore, it is the people who make or break these companies.

Companies fail and businesses are lost because honesty and prudence are not exercised in conducting the business. Consider this. We have all either heard of or had the experience of an entire plan falling apart. The following are reasons why such failures might occur:

- Honest mistakes that were a result of incorrect assumptions.
- Market or economic deterioration and collapse.
- Lack of experience on the part of the decision makers.
- Wrong skill set of the individuals who are tasked to execute the plan.
- A hidden agenda, such as a need to justify one's existence or engage in a power struggle.

The first two circumstances above can be justified and do happen. However, better evaluation and forecasting of the business environment and potential should have been done at the outset. The effects of the third and forth items on the other hand, could be very harmful; however, the situation can be quickly identified and dealt with before too much time has passed. The effects of the fifth item is the most serious and can lead to severe adverse effects on the company as a whole since it will take a long time for the truth to be uncovered. Meanwhile the damage would have already been done. This is especially true if the business plan is that of the first product of the company or is a business plan to start and establish the company, or penetrate a new market.

Take, for example, two business plans competing for a budget in a large and established company. The information in that business plan must be completely accurate and honest. No information must be withheld or omitted to influence, in any way, the views and opinions of the decision makers. It is misleading, misrepresenting, manipulating, and deceiving to do so. It is unethical. If the business plan is approved with the vital information for making the decision held back and excluded, the business plan could very well fail to deliver what it promised.

Imagine the opportunity lost and the cost to the organization. In this scenario, the funds that were approved for the deceptive business plan otherwise would have gone to fund another plan or activity that could have produced better results for the company. The opportunity cost is not only financial; it will also have an adverse impact on the personnel involved. The personnel issue, in fact, will be much more significant since it will have long-term implications for the company, its reputation and business. Think about it—if new employees are hired to work on the project outlined by the deceptive business plan, and the project fails due to a decision based on missing or inaccurate information, these employees will be perceived as having failed and they will be lost for the company as productive employees or end up getting laid off. On the other hand, when funds are assigned to the deceptive business plan instead of another plan, the employees of the other plan would be affected by not having their plan approved, leading to productivity loss, even job loss.

When it comes to procedures, extra care must be given to ensure that the procedures make sense and do not tie up the organization and its ability to conduct business by causing delays through extra layers of approvals, authorizations, and bureaucracy. Monitoring activities and progress is very important for any business; however, excessive scrutiny is like the kiss of death too. Certain managers, for example, establish procedures to approve plans or action items. As part of the control they want to exert on their team members, they require that they be kept in the loop on everything to influence the outcome.

It is important for managers to have a final say, even pull a dictator act once in a while, in such activities as budget, strategy, expenses, even some travel plans. However, some things are best delegated. It is a sign of maturity, trust, and confidence. Take, for example, determining and finalizing which customers to visit on every trip one has to make. It is perfectly acceptable for the manager and his or her team members to agree on the set of customers to visit. However, the person making the trip, who is responsible for the success of the trips and its objectives, must be trusted and well informed about the group's goals and objectives in order to be able to take the ball and run with it.

If the manager always has to interfere and interject his or her opinions and views on the trip, then the manager's trust in the employee is lacking. Either the manager is controlling or has not communicated the plans and objectives of the business to the rest of his or her team. In either case, the activity is destined for failure. During financially difficult times, it is understandable for management to scrutinize expenses, leading to overseeing travel plans and expenditure. However, this should not be the norm, nor should it be a habit. If the policies and procedures are well thought-out and defined, the process will work to the benefit of the organization, its financial health, and its employees.

Ethics in Compensation

Money Does Not Make a Good Person:
A Good Person Is One Who Uses Money to Do Good

The topic of money and compensation is a complex and sensitive one and could take a whole book to analyze and explain. In this book, however, only a few points will be addressed to establish the significance of compensation and its importance to businesses and the careers and lives of the personnel, the employees.

People's true colors show, that is, the real motives behind their decisions and actions will become known, whenever money comes into the picture. Why? Because of need or greed, satisfaction or ego, contentment vs. hunger. In business, however, there should be no place for money-driven greed and ego! There should be the desire to excel, prosper, and grow in every way. When a corporation's compensation process and standards are fair and just, good performance will result and automatically get rewarded. The compensation process, however, must begin from the start, during recruiting, and continue through the retaining process.

The real motives and agendas of money-worshipping people will eventually appear and be known, even though sometimes it will be too late to reverse the damage done by their money-driven actions and decisions; damage to the business, to the employees.

Let's make one thing clear. It is perfectly acceptable and ethical to want to make and have lots of money. However, the key is not to allow money to solely control one's decisions and one's life. When an individual makes decisions blindly and solely on the basis of making more money or having more than others, the intents will become blurred. Decisions will be tarnished and skewed rather than directed toward achieving and accomplishing the task at hand—creating good for the organization, family, friends, or whoever. The same holds true for any business entity; the business will eventually weaken and fail when most decisions are primarily money-driven, strictly bottom-line driven.

The goal of any business is to make money, making more each year than the previous year and, in the process, help the employees prosper as well. However, some of the decisions made by those in controlling and influencing positions will cause employees to expect injustices when it comes to compensation. These injustices in compensation can include these possibilities:

- Unfairness at various levels.
- Double standards.
- Manipulation.
- Favoritism.
- Deception and cheating.
- Games and politics.
- Neglect.
- Carelessness toward the employees' needs and benefits.

- Suppressed financial prosperity.
- Limiting control on financial distribution.

Consider what happened with Enron, WorldCom, and other major corporations that went bankrupt or filed for bankruptcy. While the companies were losing money and laying off their employees, the executive staff was getting enormous bonuses and perks in the millions of dollars. One thing and only one thing led to this—*greed*! Greed led to the demise of these enormous enterprises with power that influenced and impacted the economies of countries. Where were the ethics and values of these executives and what were they thinking of? They were certainly not thinking of their employees and other constituencies! They were strictly thinking of their own financial gains and that of their close circle of people.

In addition, how can anyone justify the compensation gap between various employee levels? When pay scales vary so much between different levels of an organization, between management and non-management levels, the company is basically sending the message to those on the short end of the compensation package that their contributions are not as valuable compared to those at the next level in the hierarchy. I am not implying that all employees must be paid the same. This, of course, is not realistic nor is it fair. There are employees who have many more years of experience, significantly more expertise in critical areas, higher education, or innate and intangible abilities that cannot be taught such as leadership, decision making, and the ability to give motivating speeches and presentations. However, compensation gaps should not be as great or even exist when all other qualifications are roughly equal.

It is ironic how companies tell their suppliers, "We want you to be successful and profitable so that you can continue to be in business and supply us the products and services we need," but they can't think the same way toward their own employees. The question that should be asked here is, "Why not think and feel the same way toward your own employees as well?" "Why not treat the employees in the same way you treat your suppliers?" Isn't it the same? Shouldn't the company want its employees to be prosperous and profitable, making good salaries? The answer in my mind is a definite "yes." Companies must think this way toward their employees. They need to provide them with the ability to prosper in their professional as well as their personal lives. I believe that it is the personal prosperity that wins here. When one sees that he or she is able to provide well for the family, thanks to the employer, unwavering commitment will be born within this person. No matter what or how one wants to think about money, it is a powerful force.

Etiquette of Crafting Policies and Procedures

Etiquette of Compensation

Compensation begins with clearly defined roles and responsibilities for everyone in the company, from a junior individual contributor to the executive. Then fair and appropriate compensation formulas can be crafted and offered to all employees commensurate with their roles and responsibilities, background, education, and experience. Most of us have heard the phrase "You get what you pay for." If you don't know what you are getting, how can you set a price for it? Once these roles and responsibilities are clearly defined for every position in the company, it becomes easier to implement proper compensation packages.

For new hires, the determination of the compensation package must be commensurate with the industry norms and the individual's education and experience. However, hiring managers and the human resource department must ensure that the company's approved pay scale for any position is accurately exercised and extended to new hires. If this is not done, and the employee finds out once on board—and he or she most certainly will find out—the company loses the employee's trust in the company for good and with it loses the employee's commitment.

For existing employees, the process of determining the compensation adjustment will require those who will conduct the evaluation to perform various tasks. The process of determining compensation adjustment must include the following activities:

- Determining and assigning on a company-wide basis the pool of funds available for compensation. This must be applicable to all employees. Much thought must go into determining the right qualifiers and mix of the compensation components, such as money and stock, to offer to employees based on their position, roles, and experience, guided by their performance. Even though fairness must be exercised in compensating all employees, it must also be understood that good performers and highly experienced individuals must receive more.

- Meeting with the subordinates or employees in question to discuss and clarify their roles and responsibilities.

- Outlining and defining their annual and quarterly goals and objectives. This will determine their short- and long-term goals and help them manage their time and guide their activities toward achieving their goals.

- Determining the deliverables, the results of their efforts.

- Determining when these deliverables must be completed.

- Determining how to measure the completeness of the deliverables: timeliness, accuracy, quality, effectiveness, and efficiency. This will help the employees to know exactly what is expected and it will help the managers give a fair evaluation and compensation.

- Clearly communicating that it is the individual's responsibility to determine how to go about achieving his or her tasks within predefined guidelines and that it is up to the individual to notify management of difficulties or obstacles that will stand in the way of achieving the goals and objectives. Otherwise, the individual is at fault.

- Assigning a percentage for each deliverable to identify a fully complete, partially complete, or incomplete task. This must be done at the time the goals and objective are being set.

- Adjusting the compensation and extending the offer.

Recruiting

Look Deep to Know the Person, Not Just the Resume

Flying back from Europe, I was lucky to sit next to the CEO and founder of a startup company in the networking industry headquartered in Europe. We began speaking about the industry and our careers. Finally, he asked what type of business I was doing in Europe. I told him I was there interviewing for the VP of marketing position with a large German company in the semiconductor industry. I told him that I declined the position because they wanted me to relocate to Germany. I could not relocate for personal reasons. He then told me that he was going to the states to search for and interview candidates for a VP of marketing for his company and asked if I would be interested in the position. I told him I would. We set up a time and place for the meeting with his CTO present as well.

We met the next day and had a great conversation and exchange of information. They were looking to establish an operation in the U.S. By the end of the meeting, it was clear that they really needed a general manager to establish this operation and recruit the heads of the various functional areas, including the VPs of marketing, sales, engineering, and so on. I was upfront with them about my lack of knowledge and experience in the networking and communications industry and that it would take me two to three months to acquire the necessary information about their industry and market. At this point, I posed a question to them. I asked them whether they could wait the two to three months for me to come up to speed. If they could, then I would be their man; otherwise, they would have to pass on me and search for someone from within their industry. They appreciated my openness and honesty and promised to get back to me within a week with their decision. They did get back to me with their decision, which was to pursue me. I was very pleased and honored. However, the CEO wanted to bring me on board as a consultant/contractor for six months. I thought about the offer and determined that at this stage of a startup's existence, it would be a mistake to have a contractor as the head of the operation. I told this to the CEO and added that they needed to have someone committed to the company, someone who was permanent, a full-time employee with a sense of belonging to the company. Two weeks later, the CEO offered me a permanent and full-time position as the VP and GM for the company in the U.S.

As the product and business model begin to take shape for the business entity, detailing how revenue will be generated, growing the work force must come to the forefront of all other action items. It becomes the most important activity the company can undertake because the company's success, future growth, and survival hinge on the quality of personnel it is able to recruit and retain.

In preparing for a successful recruiting process, the hiring managers must identify and understand the following crucial staffing issues:

- What is the task that needs to be performed?
- What are the skills, experience, and expertise to perform the task?
- What are the task's start and completion dates?
- How many people it will take to complete the task?

Once these four items are clearly outlined, digested, and agreed to by management, the real work of recruiting and hiring can begin. Internal and external recruiting personnel should be utilized to sift through hundreds of resumes to choose the one person who is right for the position. The two steps hiring managers must go through before contacting recruiters are as follows:

Step 1

- Draft a job description.

- Get buy-in and approval for the content of the job description from relevant parts of the company, in other words, personnel who will work side by side with the new employee who will fill this position, other managers, the human resources department, and other key personnel in other critical parts of the company.
- Identify recruiting methods, whether they are internal activities or external, such as hiring an outside recruiting firm or not.
- Determine where the new person will be physically located.
- Decide whether to search for the candidate within the company or outside.

Step 2

- Create and open a job requisition.
- Define the roles and responsibilities of the position.
- Define the qualifications of the candidate.
- Determine the title, level, and compensation package.
- Identify which organization the new employee will belong to, which manager he or she will report to, and so forth.

One key issue must be kept in mind regarding the outcomes of these two steps: there must be flexibility and the willingness to make changes, additions, and deletions until the position is filled.

As the task of searching for the right person for the position is completed, the manager's more serious tasks begin: planning how to bring the new employee up to speed within the company's environment and culture and how to retain him or her once the employee is on board. These activities will be crucial for ensuring the success and growth of the new employee and his or her ability to make long-term contributions. The preparation to ensure the growth and success of the new employee includes these activities:

- Welcoming the new employee to the company, both before and after the individual begins work.
- Recommending training programs to bring the new employee up to speed in the shortest possible time, keeping in mind the individual's experience and abilities.
- Determining when and where the new employee will be trained.
- Determining who will train the new employee.

- Outlining the long-term plans for the position as far as growth, responsibilities, attainment of new skills, additional education, and new roles; in other words, a growth path.

The information in the five items above must be clear to all involved since a good candidate will most likely ask for them. In fact, management should look for individuals who ask for these types of information and when they do, the only way to answer them is truthfully.

Having all the information listed above is necessary not only for the candidate, but is also important for the hiring manager and to the recruiters as well. For the hiring manager, the information clarifies the objectives, justifying and validating the plans for hiring a new employee with a given set of skills and responsibilities. This information is also necessary to help the manager manage more efficiently and productively. In any case, a good manager must insist on having this information complete and accurate before hiring anyone.

As to the importance of this information to recruiters, the information helps the recruiters identify and screen the right candidates and present the company accurately to the candidates. The company and its hiring manager must ensure that the recruiter is well informed and has values similar to those of the company. To the candidates, the recruiter is an extension of the company and is the front-line person for the company. Therefore it is important that the candidate's first experience with the company be the right one, the right representation. As the saying goes, "You are known by the company you keep." In this case, the company is keeping company with the recruiter who is representing it and with whom the candidate will first meet and interact. It is well known that first impressions are critical, especially in recruiting.

Companies must be certain of the position's details and clearly communicate them to the potential candidate, describing the roles and responsibilities and thus the opportunities they are offering.

However, sometimes this information is kept vague intentionally so that the candidate joins. In either case, the result and effect on the candidate are the same—devastating. Therefore, it is key for companies to do their utmost due diligence in making sure the hiring is justified and well timed and that the true situation, whatever it is, is clearly presented to the candidates.

Another matter that companies and candidates need to pay attention to is outside recruiters. These recruiters are critical to the success of the company and are an important extension of any company. They know how to reach far and deep into companies in an effort to identify and select key candidates for their clients. They are experienced in qualifying candidates' abilities and matching them to their clients' needs and requirements.

However, outside recruiters have recently become gatekeepers to the jobs that exist within companies. Companies and their managers have become too reliant and dependent on outside recruiters in general. They relinquish all the qualification activities of a candidate to the recruiter. If the recruiter and the candidate, for any number of reasons, don't click with each other, the candidate's chances of getting in front of the actual hiring manager are wiped out. No second chances are given, without regard to the fact that maybe the recruiter or candidate was off the mark that day or that the candidate might have gotten along very well with the hiring manager if the chance presented itself for the two to meet. What's worse is that some recruiters today are looking for things in candidates that have nothing to do with the candidate's abilities and qualification needed for the job outlined in the description of the position he or she is applying for. I recently read a book about executive recruiting. I was shocked by some of the criteria recruiters used to accept or decline candidates, to give them a chance to compete for the position. Written in that book were comments like, "The CEO must be over six feet tall," "not bald," "not overweight," and the like. I asked myself while reading that book, "What did these characteristics have to do with a person's abilities, qualifications, and ethical standards?" In my opinion, absolutely nothing! It is not the way you look, but what you are capable of accomplishing. Many industries have the tendency to look skin deep and do not try to get to the core of the individuals, their values and beliefs, their ethical standards and etiquette. I completely agree that appearance is very important and could influence an initial impression before the conversation begins. However, a final judgment must not be made based on first impressions and appearances alone. Many executives are perfect-looking in every way but they are failures with no character; they may even lack good ethics.

I believe it is extremely important to seek the aid of external recruiters in staffing efforts, at all levels of the organization. However, companies should have broader job descriptions for recruiters to follow that will cover not only the experience and abilities of the individual, but should also demand strength in other areas such as character, personality, and appearances too. People can lose weight, grow hair, learn how to dress for the position, or have their teeth fixed, but they cannot get taller, unfortunately. However, character traits and mental capacity, maturity and most of the human factors covered in this book are impossible to change or replace. One either has them or does not. That's where companies and their recruiters must focus.

In many societies, too much emphasis is placed on the physical appearances of individuals, company campuses and other material accessories. Long time ago I met a spiritual person who told me: "Graves have beautiful exteriors made of expensive marble and beautiful structures, carved and inscribed beautifully, but inside is only decay." He continued by saying, "Don't let appearances fool you for you could be digging your own grave."

No one suggests that beauty and appearance should be completely ignored. The issue, though, is not to let beauty rule the decision. Fairness and balance are requirements for success and prosperity.

Once the new hire is on board, two activities must take place: orientation and the game plan—setting goals and objectives—for the first three to six months. The new employee must be asked for input regarding the later point to ensure the viability of the plan. For example, if the training is planned for two months, the new hire may think it is too long or too short and should clarify why he or she thinks so.

Orientation on the other hand is to introduce the company to the new employee. It is critical for new hires and for the company itself that the company be able to present and explain vital information to the new hire. This information conveyed during orientation includes items such as the following:

- Values and beliefs.
- Mission statement.
- Vision statement.
- Business model—how the company makes money.
- Organizational structure.
- Benefits.
- Policies and procedures.
- Dos and don'ts.
- Key individuals.

During orientation, the hiring manager or one of the key colleagues of the new employee must be present during the entire orientation process. This is usually not done. In most companies where I have worked, my new manager was never present during orientation. I am just as guilty of this. However, I realized late in my career that this is one of the most important first acts for the manager and the company. This will ensure that the employee is comfortable with the information and that he or she fully understands it and buys into it. When a new hire underestimates, misinterprets, or misunderstands the information presented during orientation session, difficulties will arise for many in the company, including for the manager, the department the new hire is joining, and for the new hire him- or herself.

Many companies in the high-tech industry and in other industries no longer have orientation sessions for new hires. When they do offer them, the information and the process is so weak that it automatically undermines the importance and purpose of orientation. In some cases, the company employee who is conducting the orientation session is so passive that the new employee must ask for the information, which sometimes is not available during the session and has to be gathered and delivered to the new hire at a later date. This is the wrong representation of the company to a new hire who is expected to be motivated, committed, and productive from minute one on the job.

As much as companies must keep their long-term health and survival in mind, they must do the same for their employees and their careers. In the high-tech industry, individuals who have worked for too many companies in a short time are not viewed favorably. They are perceived as unstable and unreliable or incapable of making sound judgments about a company or career moves. Sometimes that is the case, and sometimes it is not.

In recruiting, it is crucial to relate the candidate's personal life to his or her professional life. It is important to understand what has been going on in the individual's life, personal or professional, because this will help qualify who the candidate really is. Illness, family problems, and divorce are unfortunate facts of our lives. Recruiters and hiring managers must try to understand and learn the following about candidates who went through such adversities in their lives:

- How did the candidate handle these adversities?

- What is the current situation with these problems?

- What is the current condition of the candidate, mental, emotional, and physical?

- What were the effects on the individual's professional life?

I am not suggesting that recruiters ask the candidates these questions directly since it is not legal to do so. However, they can indirectly gather the information and must use their years of experience in determining the answer to these questions and be able to access the candidates' true situation.

The opposite must also be taken into account. How did the individual's professional life impact his or her personal life? Keep in mind that we all learn and grow from our mistakes. No one is without mistakes and everyone has made a few bad or less than ideal decisions. However, it becomes unacceptable only when the same mistakes are made repeatedly.

At Company A, a director of engineering was hired. The plan for this individual was to eventually manage the entire development team. However, when hired he was positioned at the level of some of the managers who would eventually report to him. He knew this, but those managers did not. This was mistake number one. His duties were to manage the team and not to work on developing the product. This was mistake number two. One year later, he was moved to the top of the development team, the position he was originally hired for. When this happened, those managers who were at this individual's level when he was first hired were now reporting to him. They were very surprised and some were so offended that they did not want to work with him or for him. The situation got worse to the point where there would be shouting matches in meetings and hallways. Eventually these managers were not following his instructions nor paying attention to his plans. The director was finally fired.

Through no fault of his own, the director was set up for failure from the outset. The hiring managers should have envisioned the events that led to the demise of the director. The director should have been hired and placed in the position he was hired for from day one on the job. The game-playing of bringing him in at one level and moving him up later on was detected and ill feelings were created within the rest of the team toward management.

Retention

Diversity Is What Creates Newness, Progress, and Success

I was offered a position as Vice President of Sales & Marketing with a new division within Company CTI. However, before the employment offer was extended to me, a very large semiconductor firm, Company WW, extended an offer to purchase Company CTI.

This event caused two things to happen. First, the titles were adjusted downward to match the buying company's titles; second, the buying company gave the green light to the medium-sized company to continue staffing up the division they had decided to establish, which I was to join.

Four months after I joined, the Company WW requested that the new division of Company CTI should stop all its activities, especially those involving customer interactions until the merger was complete. The only thing we continued to do was to staff up the organization and conduct market research and product definition refinements.

Three months later the acquisition was completed. The first thing Company WW did was to shut down the new division, which I had joined, and transferred all the engineers to an existing and ongoing project, which Company WW was working on. The general manager of the division and I, the only non-engineers, were left without a job. It was clear that the intention of the buying company was to allow Company CTI to continue staffing the division with good engineers and have them ready to transfer to their own internal project once the acquisition was complete. Most in the new division were not only disappointed but also felt betrayed.

Once the company hires the desired individuals, the effort must shift to retaining them. Many companies go though hiring frenzies and then turn around and lay off most of those hired in a couple of years. This is irresponsible. It is not fair to play with people's lives and careers. When companies go through the hiring and layoff cycles, it is an indication of being disorganized and adrift. It is a sign of poor planning and lack of knowledge of their industry, its market, and the overall business environment. Worst of all, it causes the perception that it is an uncaring company, one that puts little value in its employees.

If a company were to go through the proper planning based on forward-looking, clear objectives, and a sound business plan, it should encounter no surprises it wouldn't be able to overcome. Even global economic downturns would not cause it to go through major layoffs every couple of years or so. The forward-looking abilities of the company should help avert any problems brought on by sudden changes in the business environment, which cause a drop in profitability or in business activities. Usually companies today lay off their employees to improve profitability or reduce cost. It is unfortunate that employee reduction is used to achieve profitability before other means are pursued and causes are identified for the lack of profitability. These companies don't think about the enormous cost of rehiring, retraining, and repeating all the efforts of bringing up new employees. The opportunity cost is huge when trying to restaff. In going through large-scale layoffs, the company's reputation will be adversely affected within its industry to the point that good people will not want to apply there for fear of being laid off at the first sign of a downturn in business. The effects of layoffs on the remaining personnel are also severe and will spill over into the work environment and business overall. The effort to avoid layoffs is part of the efforts to retain good employees.

I am not suggesting that there should be no layoffs whatsoever. There are times when cost reduction, even saving the entire company from bankruptcy, can only be achieved through work force reduction. There are also times when a product or region needs to be eliminated, in which case the employees in that region need to be let go. However, this is not the norm, but when it needs to happen it must be done with the proper etiquette, keeping those individuals' integrity intact.

It takes more effort to retain than to recruit employees because retention is a longer-term effort. When recruiting, the company puts out the right image to attract candidates:

- Position.
- Title.
- Compensation package.
- Products and target markets.
- Reputation.
- Profitability.
- Physical location and campus.

Figure 13 illustrates the external image companies put out to attract and recruit good candidates. The messages and reputation are communicated to the outside world, to its industry, to better compete for good individuals.

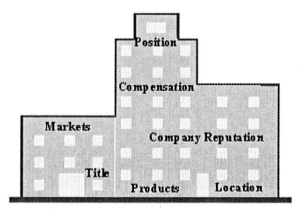

Figure 13 Recruiting—the company's exterior image

However, when the effort is to retain employees, the company must do more to ensure that the right motivating elements are present for the employee to stay with the company and they include:

- Compensation.
- Potential for growth, in all areas.
- Promotion.
- Effective management.

- Company policies.
- Quality of communication.
- Company culture.
- Prosperity.
- Facilitation and promotion of a balanced life.

Mismanaged companies seem to fail when it comes to retaining their employees.

Therefore, once the new employee is inside, the efforts must change to one of retaining him or her. It is no longer about messages and image. It is about the treatment and opportunity the new employee will receive. Feelings of contentment and prosperity, fair challenges, growth, respect and work environment are the factors that will retain employees. Figure 14 highlights some of the factors that will help the company retain employees.

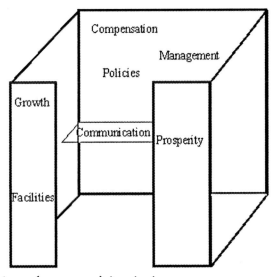

Figure 14 Retention—the company's interior image

The Wisdom in What I Learned

Policies, Like Ethics, Define the Right Things to Do; Procedures, Like Etiquette, Outline the Right Way of Doing Them

Policies and Procedures Protect People and Business

Money Does Not Make a Good Person: A Good Person Is One Who Uses Money to Do Good

Look Deep to Know the Person, Not Only the Resume

Diversity Is What Creates Newness, Progress and Success

Chapter Eight

Product Creation

The Quality of a Company's Products Defines Its Set of
Values and Beliefs and Vice Versa

The main purpose for establishing any business entity is to generate revenue through the sale of products, services, or both. However, without mentally, emotionally, and physically healthy personnel, products cannot be defined, developed, manufactured, sold, or supported.

Let's say an individual has an idea for a product that he or she believes will be in great demand and achieve great success. This individual will recruit others with the right skill sets to build the team that will make this product idea a reality or, if a team already exists, then the process of creating the product is ready to begin. From this point onward each thought, each decision, each action must be taken with high ethics and etiquette in mind.

Consider this. A product is defined to satisfy a need, serve a purpose, or solve a problem. Therefore, one can assume that it is to do good—financial, medical, educational, environmental, technological, or humanitarian good. Thus, the process of defining and creating a product must be conducted ethically and with purely good intentions to reflect that goodness. Keep in mind the phrase "You get out what you put in." Put in goodness and you'll get goodness. Put in garbage and you'll get a mess.

Ethics in Product Creation

Keep People in Mind When Defining and Producing Products

The process for defining and creating new products must include certain beliefs and practices to meet the highest ethical standards. The practices needed to define and create healthy products include the following:

1. Do not define or create products to justify a position or a group's existence. Every product must be able to survive and succeed on its own without being a burden on other products if and when the product were to fail.

2. Do not define products to justify expanding an organization at the expense of another. Define and develop products that will expand the entire company, its revenue and personnel. Your product will be well served then by the entire company and its personnel. People want to be part of a winner.

3. The truth always comes out sooner or later. Prepare a business or justification plan ensuring accurate, fair, and true content.

4. The products must satisfy the organization, its personnel, and the target customers or users, creating a win-win scenario for all. The satisfaction could be financial, moral, and so on.

5. Products must not pose danger to anyone or anything, inside or outside the company, such as the environment or people.

6. Outline realistic schedules and milestones. Unrealistic schedules create unrealistic expectations that lead to strains on the relationships with constituents and a deteriorating work environment. If too short of a timeline, for example, is presented and the schedule is not met, for whatever reason, everyone involved in the project could be in jeopardy or their reputation adversely affected.

7. Present realistic and honest product sales and revenue forecasts. Unrealistic projections will lead to erroneous hiring plans and budgets. When the expectations are not met, layoffs and a drop in the company's valuation will occur. This happens for several reasons; for example, expansion plans may have been made according to the revenue that was going to be generated by the new product.

8. Get the job done with existing tools unless they are inefficient or outdated. In other words, be cost conscious.

9. Know when to modify the project or pull the plug and cancel.

Keep this in mind: you will perform at your best when the values and benefits of the products you define or work on match your own values and beliefs. Defining, creating, and producing products involve more things than just raw material and labor. These are the tangibles that go into the makeup of the product. In addition to these tangibles, there are the intangibles that are more critical and have much more impact on the success of the product and its long-term impact on the company and society.

Figure 15 identifies the intangibles that go into the makeup of any product. Much of what a product is reflects what the developer or designer puts into it, in other words, the type of person the developer is. The intangibles that go into the creation of a product include the following:

- The human elements. The care with which the product is conceived, defined, and produced. Includes passion, respect, desire, excitement, joy, pride and the quality of the developers.

- Ethics and values. The impact the product will have on the company producing the product, its users, and society.

- Thoughts and creativity. The brainpower that created the product.

- Information. All relevant information about the market, competition, specifications, customers, and so on that will go into the makeup of the product.

- Planning. The tactical steps that will lead to the creation of the physical product.

- Mental organization. The sequence of organized mental thoughts that outline the events that will lead to the product conception, development, creation, and production.

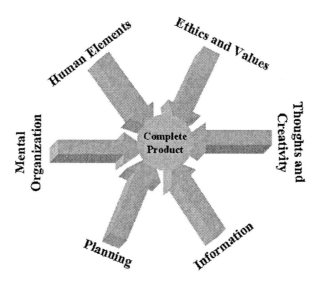

Figure 15 The intangibles of a product

On the other hand, when the intangibles are left out of the makeup of any product, the company's resulting products or the effects of the products can leave a negative impact on people, society, and the environment. We have all heard news about companies that produced toxic substances, material and products, and how they were identified and penalized years later. However, the truth was not uncovered until many suffered, financially and physically. Afterward, the company, and sometimes the entire industry, was penalized at a cost far greater than if they had resorted to safer products and practices to begin with. Perfect examples are companies in the tobacco, oil, and chemical industries. Some of the products these industries produce are vital to many other industries and to many people.

When the processes and methods used by companies to produce their materials take into account the health of the environment they live and operate in, the result will be fabulous—a safe and healthy environment. When care is not taken in producing some of these products and the only result sought is financial gains, the bottom line, the outcome is usually devastating to everyone involved including, sooner or later, the company itself. Perfect examples of dangerous by-products to the environment are

- The discharge of toxins into the air, the ground, or bodies of water;
- Effects on the health of individuals using the toxic product;
- Cars that do not use fuel efficiently.

Products do not define, design, and develop themselves. People, the employees of companies, do. Therefore, it is paramount to use the highest ethical standards to implement these processes; otherwise, these employees and their employer must be held accountable and they usually are. In many cases, the wrong practices of producing the product or the adverse effects of using them are made public by the company's own employee, or a group of employees. The employees' conscience could not bear to see the results produced by these products nor did it allow them to remain silent. In many cases, these individuals risked their own employment, well-being, even their lives in doing the right thing, by coming out into the open in an attempt to protect society and the environment. The outcome of producing such harmful products turns out to be very costly to a number of entities:

- Individual companies.
- The industry as a whole, such as the tobacco industry.
- Insurance companies who have to pay out large amounts of money to cover lawsuits.
- Government resources to resolve and deal with the particular problem. Sometimes these resources are scarce or would have otherwise been deployed for other more fruitful tasks.
- The local, state, or national economy.
- Community. The ultimate losers are the people, the families and whole communities where the company operates and produces its products. This is especially true if the community has to relocate due to severe contamination of the ground and water or if the company has to shut down its operation, causing the loss of jobs and wages, and leading to the eventual demise of the community.

Once businesses experience some of the events mentioned above, reality sets in and efforts begin to reverse the damage, if it is not too late. They realize that the cost of developing a harmful product is greater than the cost of taking the right steps and following the right processes in the right way from the outset, in other words, following the ethical way of doing things with the good of the people in mind. In some cases following the ethical way of defining and producing the products might have cost more, initially, than the other ways, but in the long run the cost would be less after taking all the risks into account. I don't mean to paint a dark picture, but this is the truth. Whenever the contribution of a product to the bottom line is the only and main objective to be achieved at all costs by a business entity, the results are usually grim and harmful. This is also true for cutting corners in the development and production of a product only to save time and money, not paying attention to the final outcome.

The main question to be asked is "Where did the process go wrong?" The answer is that the mistakes took place in the definition stage of the product and during the steps that had to be taken to produce it. Who envisioned, thought, and planned? The answer is an employee or a group of employees. Sometimes, the creators of product ideas propose their ideas to the companies they work for at the time but the idea is rejected for a variety of reasons. One of those reasons could be the values and beliefs, the ethical standards, the company stands for, will not allow it to participate in such a product activity.

The employee then goes elsewhere and keeps on trying until one company accepts his or her idea and the disastrous cycle begins. Usually the company accepting the idea does so for competitive status and financial gains. They do not evaluate all the ramifications of accepting that product idea. This is the reason why industry-monitoring organizations exist. Unfortunately, some of these bodies are industry-run and their actions and decisions are influenced and directed by the industry they are intended to monitor.

Granted, sometimes, the mistakes are unintentional. Sometimes the results and outcomes could not have been known at the product's inception. However, if and when the problems are detected, the process has to be changed and corrected, not covered up. In addition, those individuals who come forward must be rewarded for their contributions in averting a potentially disastrous situation and outcome.

Product Creation Etiquette

Be True to Your Decisions

So what is the right process, the etiquette, to define a product? The answer varies from one product to the next, from one company to the next and from one industry to the next. However, there are a few common steps that must be followed to define and produce the right product:

1. Talking to target customers and users.
2. Evaluating the competing products.
3. Identifying all the material needed to produce the product.
4. Identifying all the byproducts that will be produced by the original product.
5. Analyzing every step of the product fabrication process.
6. Identifying all the right people within the company and sharing and discussing the findings of steps 4 and 5 above with each and every one of them.
7. Revisiting the product idea after completing discussions with the right people inside and outside the company.
8. Presenting the formalized product idea to one or two key and trustworthy customers and or partners to get their feedback
9. Continuously monitoring the product during its development and fabrication stages to ensure that all is right and according to plan.
10. Thinking, planning, and implementing ethically.

A strong and committed team must exist behind a successful product. This team must have experience, knowledge, and expertise to complete the tasks and perform the due diligence required.

The product team does not need to be large. Initially only four to five individuals from different functional areas will suffice. The functional areas that must be represented are engineering, marketing, sales, finance, and operations or manufacturing. In some cases, a representative from the sales organization should not be included as a member of the team. This is the team that is going to conceive, define, and oversee the introduction of the product.

In addition, a senior manager or executive should be assigned to support the team in facilitating progress and removing obstacles that the rest of the product definition team may encounter. These obstacles could be lack of resources, lack of commitment from other parts of the organization, or lack of experience about how certain corporate functions work and so forth.

The role of each of the functional areas represented in the product definition team must be well outlined and understood by the team members. The following is a brief description of the roles of each functional area in defining and creating the product:

Marketing

- Produce the product idea, solely or in collaboration.
- Create the straw-man proposal outlining the draft, high-level features and performance criteria of the product. This proposal is in the form of a presentation that will be presented to management and very few select customers, two to three at most.
- Identify the target market and target customers.
- Identify the competition and existing competitive solutions.
- Create a complete marketing plan. It must include a Marketing Requirement Document (MRD) and a Product Requirement Document (PRD), revenue and growth projections.
- Create the product family road map, that is, follow-on and derivative products to the first product in the family.

Engineering

- Produce the product idea, solely or in collaboration.
- Verify the technology.
- Validate the feasibility of developing such a product.
- Qualify development expertise needed and is available within the company and outside.
- Determine the product development timeline, or schedule.
- Determine the cost.

Finance

- Set price and margin guidelines.

Operations/Manufacturing

- Identify the manufacturing processes to be used.
- Determine the manufacturing cost of the product.

- Identify or select a manufacturer if the company does not have manufacturing capability.
- Ensure testability of the product.
- Provide delivery schedules and production lead times.

Sales

- Evaluate sales team participation on a case-by-case basis and dependant on the level of experience and workload.
- Produce or validate the product idea.
- Introduce product definition team to the customers.
- Provide market data and feedback, such as customer base, competition, pricing targets, lead time.
- Manage relations with customers who receive the initial proposal. Those customers are sometimes called "early adopters."

Once the product is defined and its features and performance specifications set, the product development can begin. During the product development period, ongoing monitoring of the data gathered must be conducted and new findings communicated to all team members. Updates and progress reports must be communicated weekly within the product development community and monthly, or as needed, to other members of the other functional areas involved in the product definition and development, including senior and executive management.

Involvement of the higher management and executive levels will be determined according to the complexity and criticality of the product to the company as a whole. In some cases, the CEO may be involved on a quarterly basis or as the CEO deems necessary. Communicating the progress and updates of the product development is done through various meetings, for example:

- Cross-functional meetings, with attendees from various functions, such as engineering and marketing
- Functional meetings, with attendees who perform the same function, such as engineering. These functional meetings address specific activities that must take place within that function, such as design review, design tools requirements, design problems, and difficulties
- Other types of meetings, including product-planning meetings, marketing update meetings, operations meetings, and forecast meetings, will take

place to communicate valuable information to the rest of the team. The team will adjust their activities based on these new pieces of information.

As you can see, to define and produce a product involves many people, many steps, and many types of materials. Keep in mind, though, that the makeup of a product includes both tangible and intangible components and all must be ethical and with the proper etiquette.

The Wisdom in What I Learned

The Quality of a Company's Products Defines Its Set of Values and Beliefs and Vice Versa

Keep People in Mind When Defining and Producing Products

Be True to Your Decisions

You Will Get Out What You Put In

Part Three

Humanizing the Corporation

Respect Is the First Step on the Ladder of Success

Chapter Nine

The Forgiving Company

The Practice of Tolerance and Understanding

Forgiveness Creates Commitment and Sacrifice

In 1994 my wife of fifteen years was diagnosed with cancer and was given a maximum of twenty-four months to live. During her battle for her life, I was trying to fight career battles, in addition to giving her as much support as possible and caring for our two children.

With my attention spread out, my focus was weakened. I missed important cues about what was going on in the company I worked for at the time. I missed things like corrupt behavior in the company I worked for, better career opportunities at other companies, and industry trends in general. Consequently I did not pursue better and higher-level management position opportunities that were available to people with my experience and skill set. The result was that between 1994 and 2002 I worked for seven companies, many of which went out of business, causing me to make rapid changes.

After leaving the company I had been with since 1994, I joined a company in early 1997. After joining I found out that I had been misled about the position I was to hold in a new division within the company. Eight months later I resigned and joined another company, which was bought five months after I joined, and the division I joined was disbanded. However, I was offered a position to relocate, but due to my wife's condition, I could not accept and had to resign.

Within the next two years I joined three companies, all of which went out of business. The following two years I spent searching for a new career opportunity. However, the companies I spoke with were concerned about my short stays with the last five employers—five companies in five years. That was the item they pointed to before anything else. The recruiters and hiring managers alike were asking the same questions, "Why were you there for such a short time?" "What happened at company X?" and so on. No matter what I said or how many details I provided them with regarding the reasons, I was not pursued. What influenced the decisions of these hiring managers were the short stays and not what I had accomplished or the experience I had gained.

At first, I did not mention anything about the effects of my personal life on my ability to focus and make sound decisions. But I began noticing that no one was trying to understand and appreciate what had happened and why. So, I began sharing openly the professional and personal reasons for my moves. To my surprise and disappointment, even that did not seem to make a difference even though I handled all that was dealt to me and came out of it in good shape, mentally, emotionally, and physically.

It seems that we find it much easier to put up with and forgive people in our personal lives than in our professional lives. When friends, relatives, family members, even strangers, do something that is unacceptable to us for whatever reason, most of the time they are forgiven or just ignored. Yes, there is a limit for how much we are willing to tolerate, but usually the incident is forgotten and forgiven. However, when the same thing happens in the workplace it seems to be much more difficult for us to forgive and forget. The reason for this is that it is perceived that all mistakes in business cost the business money and put the business on a dangerous footing. However, this is not the case!

Of course, there are various types of mistakes with different levels of adverse effects. There are mistakes that are made out of mischief or carelessness, and some that are due to inexperience or incompetence. I will call the latter two "white mistakes" along the lines of "white lies." Again, white mistakes are due to incompetence, limited knowledge, or inexperience. They are harmful and can cost the business entity revenue and credibility and should not be tolerated. However, they must be addressed by understanding the individual's abilities, circumstances and overall environment. White mistakes by employees are due to various factors:

- Mental or physical exhaustion.
- Poor judgment or underestimation.
- Wrong decisions.
- Lack of experience and expertise.
- Sudden and temporary difficulty in one's personal life or environment.

As I mentioned earlier, I am drawing parallels between white mistakes and white lies, which everyone has told, has heard of, understands, and in most cases accepts. So if white lies are accepted, why shouldn't the same treatment be given to white mistakes? In my opinion, most white lies are much worse than white mistakes and can cause much more damage. A lie is a lie, large or small. It is intentional and damaging because its intention is to help the individual who is lying get away with something. Usually those who tell so-called small lies will graduate to big lies. It becomes a habit.

In the case of white mistakes, they are unintentional and those who make them will never graduate to intentional mistakes, unless the individuals are corrupt. No ethical person with good integrity and self-respect would want to make mistakes on purpose. Usually, the mistakes are corrected and are never repeated. It is therefore, crucial that when such mistakes are uncovered and encountered, tolerance and understanding are extended to protect the integrity of the individual and that of the business entity, helping both to reach excellence.

"Every one has and will make mistakes." "No one is perfect." We all have heard these statements and have spoken them ourselves. However, on many occasions they are used when it is convenient. If these statements were meant when used, then those who were guilty of making the mistake wouldn't be ridiculed and reprimanded repeatedly. However, we have become unforgiving and unforgetting, thus creating organizations and companies that are unforgiving and unforgetting as well. The actions taken against those who have made white mistakes are numerous:

- Not offering employment.
- Not extending a good compensation package.
- Isolating the individual.
- Reducing responsibilities and authority.
- Labeling and judging.
- Removing privileges.
- Humiliating the individual.
- Making an example of the individual and the mistake.

These acts are carried out in business, in sports, in politics, and other fields.

Figure 16 illustrates how forgiveness creates positive outcomes that will elevate the entire organization to a new level of success and prosperity leading to loyalty and commitment. Once loyalty and commitment are established within any company, the sky will be the limit for the successes that can be achieved.

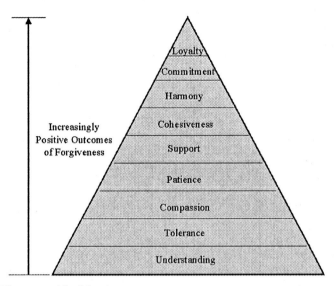

Figure 16 The pyramid of forgiveness

There is nothing as healing and as powerful as the act of forgiving. In business or in personal life, forgiving is the source of tolerance and understanding. When tolerance is present, so will compassion, patience, and support. With these characteristics present, there will be harmony, cohesiveness, prosperity, and success for any business entity and its personnel because it will prove that business and people are one.

Many companies, even entire industries, tend to be unforgiving and unforgetting of past mistakes, white mistakes or otherwise, made by industry professionals. For example, it is not viewed favorably when an individual shows on his or her resume that he or she worked for two or three companies in, say, three or four years. Regardless of the reasons for the short stays, the individual is viewed as unreliable, unstable and untrustworthy. When a hiring manager sees this information, he or she immediately assumes that the applicant is at fault, even if the background and experience are exactly in line with what the company is looking for and all the references are impeccable. It almost seems like a punishment when professionals are not even given an opportunity to explain glitches or missteps in their career paths.

This judgmental attitude could be very dangerous in the business world. A black-or-white style of thinking could cost companies dearly in losing good candidates and damaging their business. Yes, there should be a limit to how often one changes his or her employer, but it is just as important to determine and understand the reasons for the changes if the candidate's qualifications are a good fit. In many cases, the job changes were not under the control of the individual.

There are numerous reasons for individuals to change their employer:

- Incompatibility with the company culture.
- Poor company performance.
- Management style difference with the immediate manager.
- Layoffs.
- Company going out of business.
- Lack of upward mobility.
- The prospect of gaining better responsibilities and compensation, say, over 25 percent higher than current compensation. This is not applicable to certain positions and cannot be justified every time.
- Poor products or lack of products at the current company.
- Geographic location.
- Family and personal reasons.
- The need for more challenging position and responsibilities.

All of these and many other reasons can contribute to good professionals, good performers, deciding to change their job. We have all done it, some more than others, but the industry and decision makers choose to ignore that and immediately jump to negative conclusions, blaming the applicant. It is much healthier to have an open mind toward situations and people. It is ironic, though, how many companies tend to selectively forgive some of their employees, especially in their executive ranks, for past failures and less than desirable performances. Take CEOs for example. They join one company and end up under performing or, in some cases, damaging the business yet they seem to get better and better offers and positions with other companies after they are let go by the latest employer. I remember when working for Company SC, we had a highflying CEO who everyone thought would be a savior for the company. However, he turned out to be a big spender that was mostly talk. After being let go from Company SC, he ended up at even a more prestigious company as the CEO. In less than 2 years he was asked to leave.

However, those same companies find it difficult to be forgiving of a potentially new recruit. There has to be evenhandedness in one's actions, no double standards. It is human nature to take care of and forgive one of your own, but loyalty from within grows when others, from the outside, are also helped and forgiven through fairness.

After all, it is people we are talking about here. As I have stated repeatedly companies are not just buildings and desks, chairs and books. A company is its people. People, in general, want to see people succeed. For people to succeed, they will need different kinds of support or assistance. The type of support or assistance will depend on the individual's abilities and resources. When a company understands and appreciates an individual's circumstances, and moves toward forgiveness, offering a chance to succeed, the company becomes *humanized*. A company is its people and by enabling the people to act and become involved, the company becomes humanized. It is a reflection on the company's employees, their values, and character. When this happens, a sense of unity, camaraderie, and completeness takes over the entire organization, and leads to a cohesive team that will create success.

The Wisdon in What I Learned

Forgiveness Creates Commitment and Sacrifice

A Caring and Forgiving Company Is A Humanized Company.

Chapter Ten

Mutual Respect for the Self and for Others

Respect in Order to be Respected

Working at Company OK, as VP of marketing and sales, I had the opportunity to develop strong relationships with customers all around the world. I took every opportunity to do so to develop long-lasting relationships based on trust, respect, and openness. One such customer was a very large European company in the consumer electronics industry.

Of course, when developing a relationship with a company, one is really developing the relationship with one or more individuals who work for the company. I established a relationship with the buyer. He was a very shrewd negotiator, which was a good thing for his company. However, even though he was tough, he conducted the negotiations with class, with understanding and respect for my company's position and me.

Unfortunately, I never won his business while with Company OK. My product's timing and price did not fall inline with his needs. We continued to be in touch with one another and had several meetings and communications whenever one of us was in the other's territory. However, the time came when I had to leave my position with Company OK. The company I joined afterwards, Company M, was in the same space as Company OK, and this European company was one of my new employer's target customers to win. However, my Company M had tried to win this customer but without success. In fact, the European company was not pleased with my new employer. I found out later on that the reason for this was that Company M had made many promises and commitments that were not kept.

I decided to take a stab at it. I called my contact, the buyer in the European company. We immediately connected with each other and began catching up on non-business matters. When we got to the business issues, I was able to understand his concerns and frustration and promised that I would address the issues and get back to him. I did that and kept my promise to him. This led to a face-to-face meeting at his company site in Europe. We then followed up with a management meeting that resulted in a large engineering session, which resulted in a multimillion-dollar business win for Company M and an entry into the market it was targeting to penetrate. All this was the result of the buyer's and my appreciation and respect for one another, our companies, and our businesses.

The title of this chapter spells it out. You have to respect yourself to have the capacity and willingness to respect others. Again, the word etiquette is defined as "the forms and practices prescribed by social convention or by authority to be observed in social or official life." The parallel here is that when there is respect, etiquette will be present, and when there is etiquette, respect is present. It is the respect for things accepted and prescribed to by society, in personal and professional life.

In business, as I mentioned earlier in this book, to succeed there must be a two-way-street mentality between the employer and the employee. Two key questions have been asked many times by so many and have produced the same answer time after time. These two questions are, "What does the company we work for want and expect from us?" and "What do we want and expect from the company we work for?" The fundamental answers to both questions are and should be *respect!*

Let's take the employer first. With respect, the employer demonstrates the following to the employees:

- Care for their personal and professional lives.
- Value for their comfort, which means providing good amenities and equipment they use to do their work.
- Value for their well-being as well as that of their families.
- Value for their prosperity, financial and otherwise.
- Value for itself to ensure that its employees are well cared for so that it will succeed in all its endeavors.

The exact same items listed above will result when employees respect their employer. It is all about mutual respect.

All previous chapters addressed the issue of how businesses should treat employees, how employees should be respected as a show of the company's respect for what it stands for and what it wants to achieve. Respect must be shown to every employee, from the janitor to the chief executive officer—no exceptions. When this is achieved, unity will be established.

Consider the following: a small twig is thin and frail and can be easily broken in half by anyone, young or old. Now, take ten or twenty of those twigs, wrap them up with a string, and then try to break them. Mostly likely they will not be easy to break. Why? Because when these twigs are put together, they become strong as a whole. They become one unit. There is strength in numbers. The same holds true of any business entity. Through the unity of its employees and their mission, guided by respect for each other, successes will be achieved by the business entity.

Respect is not only about being polite and using such words as "please" and "thank you." It is much bigger than words alone. It is a way of thinking about things, a way of viewing things, a way of approaching things, a way of treating, and a way of behaving. It is a way of existing with other people and other things. In conducting ourselves in our daily lives, professional or personal, we must consider how our actions and spoken words, affect the people around us and, in some cases, all things around us. Our conduct will also affect the results we seek and it includes the way we live, speak, think, interact, dress, sit, eat, drink and so forth.

Take rudeness, for example. It is the result of poor manners and disrespect. Rudeness comes in many forms and is displayed through various behaviors including coarse language, impolite interaction, inappropriate posture, poor eating habits, excessive drinking, inappropriate attire, and so on. When it comes to business, it seems that we lose what we were taught at a young age. We were taught not to be rude, to be polite, to say things like "thank you," "please," "may I help you," "what would you like," "would you mind helping me," and so forth. As I write these phrases, they sound and feel good. I wonder where these phrases are now. They seem to have disappeared from the vocabulary of most professionals. In personal life, most people still use these phrases regularly, but they are fading away in business.

How many meetings have you attended where the conversation was so rude and vulgar that it's a surprise a fight did not break out? Sometimes when getting into your office you greet people in the lobby or passing by but you don't get a reply. Managers rudely tell you to get something for them, sometimes without a please or thanks. We all are guilty of having done some of these acts. However, the issue is that now these acts happen all the time and they are becoming an accepted norm. Rudeness is not only verbal. It is expressed physically as well; for example, people put their feet on the table or desk when sitting across from a colleague, even when the other person is eating. These acts should be neither acceptable nor tolerated.

At Company SC people used to brag about the fact that they went to meetings and chewed someone out. One of my colleagues actually resigned from a good position he was holding due to the effects of the constant confrontational and argumentative environment in meetings on his health. "The meetings were cruel," he'd say, "full of personal attacks and destructive behavior."

Nothing was getting done, resulting in wasted time, money, and productivity. It was no wonder that that company had more problems retaining its good people and customers than did its competitors. Layoffs occurred every twelve to eighteen months. The funny thing was that management always wondered why the company was in such poor condition. People were unhappy, the atmosphere was dull, and nothing was working, nothing. I left that company after being there for two years, and my friend eventually had a heart attack. Imagine how powerful the effects of such behavior must be to do this to a healthy person who was previously a member of the U.S. Armed Forces. He did recover from the heart attack, but that period was very hard on him and his family.

Rude behavior and poor manners have even more serious and damaging side effects when the culprit is a manager. When a manager misbehaves, the ill effects of the behavior will be felt by his or her entire team and a chain reaction will take place.

Let's keep in mind one very important thing; there should be no difference between the way we act with people inside or outside of the workplace. People are people, everywhere. Employees must think and act the same way toward the employees of the company they work for, as they do with employees of other companies, including those working for their competitors. Most importantly however, is for the individuals to respect themselves, to have self-respect. It is only then that those individuals are able to respect others and this is the foundation on which respect for things is built. An industry is similar to the globe, planet earth. Just as the world is made up of many countries, most of which are striving to live in order and mutual respect, so is an industry. It is made up of many companies that must coexist with complete respect toward one another.

To show respect, one must consider the audience, paying careful consideration and attention to the nationality, race, religion, ethnic background, gender, age, customs, habits, needs, requirements, and motives of all the audience. A cookie-cutter approach will no longer work in business! Proper ethics and etiquette will touch every aspect of the business entity. Ethics are at the core of every successful individual and every successful company because they touch every element of the business. Etiquette is just as important as ethics—it, too, touches every component and aspect of the individual and the business.

Figure 17 illustrates how ethics touch every aspect of the business entity because they affect an individual's professional and personal existence and conduct. Ethics is then the core from which everything sprouts, good or bad, personal or professional. Etiquette, though, has two components, business or professional, etiquette and personal etiquette. They are influenced by one another and are inseparable. However, notice that the etiquette is the shell that eventually wraps up the makeup of the individual. It is, in a sense, the icing on the cake. Etiquette puts a nice wrapper on ethics and presents it to the rest of the world.

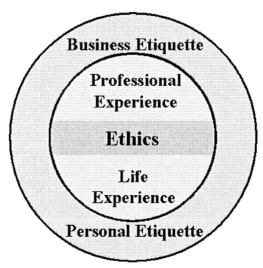

Figure 17 The relationship between ethics and etiquette

We no longer live in a closed and isolated society. With the explosive growth of travel and communications capabilities such as the Internet and cellular phones, the world has suddenly shrunk, becoming a very small place. People's ability to reach, influence, and affect other people in different parts of the globe has increased dramatically. Therefore, it is crucial for business people to practice respect and use the proper ethics and etiquette in conducting themselves and their business.

In conducting business and dealing with business professionals in other parts of the world, nothing should be taken for granted. No assumptions should be made. It is not acceptable to do or say something just because that is the way one is used to doing or saying it or because it is something that is done or said where one comes from. One should not try to impose his or her own way of doing things onto others, particularly onto present or future business constituents. Remember, "Do to others as you want done to you." Better yet, "Don't do to others what you don't want done to you." All that's needed is to act with respect and good intentions; if the people you do business with or are planning to do business with feel that what you offer is right for them as well, they will pick it up without extra effort on your part. Of course, one must try one's best to convince the potential client or partner; however, the efforts must be true and proper.

Remember, you are dealing with people. Communicate and conduct yourself with proper ethics and etiquette, and you'll see that things will unfold in your favor, meeting all the goals and objectives that have been set for you and your business entity.

As I already mentioned, we were taught from early childhood to show respect to others. However, some of what we were taught seems to have either slipped away permanently or slips away when we are conducting business. Sometimes our manners selectively slip away when it is convenient for us.

Insults and intimidations through the use of certain words or vocal tones are recipes for disaster in any situation. Eventually the disaster will strike and those who insult could be on the receiving end. Many land mines can be encountered during conversations with people from other cultures, such as:

- Calling someone by his or her first name.
- Interrupting others during their speech.
- Using rude or impolite language.
- Acting obnoxiously and talking loudly.

I stated in an earlier chapter the importance of both written and verbal communication. However, there is another aspect to communication and that is the physical aspect. When we communicate with others, we are interacting with them, and here, the importance of the physical aspects of communication come into play, such as:

- Gestures.
- Touch. In some cases and in some cultures it is acceptable to touch the elbow of the person, tap the shoulder or even hug and or kiss. On the other hand, in other cultures touching of any kind is unacceptable, period. Therefore, it is very important to know to whom, when, and where this behavior would be acceptable, based on knowledge of the culture and background.
- Personal space. Where to be situated relative to the other person or persons you are speaking to: how near or far, next to, behind or in front of, near a door, or facing the door.
- Eye contact. There is a belief in some cultures that says "Don't trust a person who does not look you in the eye when talking to you." Eyes give away a lot of information without using words. In Western cultures, people who don't make eye contact usually either lack self-confidence in what they are saying or have a hidden agenda or motive.

- Dining. Conversing while having a meal is where most mistakes are made. This will be covered shortly.

During interaction with others, behaviors surface that could make or break any business deal or even the start of a business relationship. We must be impeccable in our behavior if we want to succeed. The individual's behavior demonstrates what he or she is all about—whether he or she is honest, respectful, confrontational, aggressive, and so forth. It is a measure and an indicator to others as to whether the individual is reliable, trustworthy, refined enough for them to do business with or not, intelligent, and so forth. Some of the behaviors that indicate who and what the person is all about include the following:

- Projecting self-confidence.
- Paying attention.
- Seriousness.
- Acting with responsiveness and enthusiasm.
- Listening.
- Concentration.
- Being participative and energetic.

When our behavior is out in the open, so will the thoughts behind our behavior, such as:

- What do we think about the individuals we are conversing with?
- What do we think about the concepts or topics being discussed or presented?
- How knowledgeable are we about the subject matter being discussed or about matters in general?

- How open and receptive are we to others or to new views and opinions different from ours?
- How sincere are we in our answers and replies?
- How do we answer questions and respond to comments?

Again, if you think about the above, you can deduce that they are all connected to respect and intent; respect for the self and respect for others, and the intent to do good.

How we appear to others and to ourselves, in other words, how we dress, move, stand, walk, and sit, all lead to the same point: respect for the self and for others. Consider this: Why do people buy new outfits, suits and dresses, shirts and blouses, shoes and ties when they are ready to go to a wedding or a holiday party, for example? Because it has a feel-good effect on the individuals themselves and on the people around them. It is also an indication of one's self-respect and respect for others and for the occasion. However, appropriateness has to be exercised.

Appearance has to fit the role, the position, the surrounding environment, the culture, and the occasion. Even if we don't care for a suit-and-tie look, we have to play the role in certain situations because that is what those we are interacting with require or expect out of people they want to do business with, based on cultural or personal custom or habit. For example, in meetings with bankers or large traditional corporations people are expected to wear suits and ties, a conservative look. These don't have to be the latest statements in fashion, but appropriate attire is required. In the high-tech industry on the other hand, both casual attire and formal, suit-and-tie looks are acceptable. Companies in parts of Europe, Latin America, Asia, Japan, and the Middle East, for example, are more formal than those in the U.S. A tie is a minimum requirement in those places.

However, wearing formal and appropriate attire is not enough. The condition of the attire must be acceptable as well. If, for instance, the attire is not properly pressed, is not clean, or if the person's hair is a mess or beard unshaven, the effects are just as bad as if the entire attire was wrong for the culture or occasion. Therefore, the total appearance is important.

Consideration must also be given to the individual's attire as it relates to the position of those he or she will interact with, such as managers, executives, individual contributors, bankers, or landlords. Decision makers must be positively influenced in total and in every way for the individual and the business to succeed. I am not talking about a façade, but a respectful and appropriate look.

This is limited not only to physical appearance, but also to mental disposition as well.

When I purchased my first house, I was short of cash. I borrowed money from family and promised to pay it back in one year. To pay this loan, I held a second job in the evenings, working for a high-end men's clothing store. I was an engineer in the mornings and a retail salesman in the evenings and weekends. On Mondays, business used to be very slow. All of us working one Monday evening, including the manager on duty, were at the counter shooting the breeze. A customer finally walked in. He had on a worn-out pair of jeans and a shirt that was not tucked in. Everyone thought, no money, no sale, no time for this guy. After approximately 15 minutes, while I was watching this customer check out some accessories, shirts and ties, I decided to approach him. Actually, I felt bad for him being ignored by all of us. Within 30 minutes, this customer chose $800 worth of shirts and ties. I carried the merchandise to the counter for him. When it was time for this customer to pay, the store manager wanted identification, not believing that a person who looked like this could have a platinum credit card. His credit card was approved, and he walked out of the store happy and so was I. The moral of the story is: "Don't assume, don't judge, and most importantly, don't let looks deceive you and blur your vision."

Another one of the important components of proper conduct is to know how to sit. Sitting can communicate many things about the person and his or her disposition regarding the event at hand. It is also a strong indicator of the level of respect the individual has toward others who are present. Sometimes the behavior is unintentional, but still the resulting effects can be the same as if it were. For example, sitting upright on the front half of the seat indicates attentiveness and alertness. However, sinking all the way back in the chair indicates or could be perceived as a lack of interest or laziness. When sitting casually, usually most people cross their legs. Men usually rest the ankle of one leg on the knee of the other leg, or knee over knee. However, one must be sensitive to the environment and the people who are present before deciding which method is appropriate and which is not.

Usually in business, it is unacceptable, unless the individuals know each other very well, to cross the legs with ankle over knee. This is especially true in Europe and the Middle East where it is considered an insult for those cultures and for different reasons.

In the Middle East, for example, it is an insult to the person to have the bottom of the shoe of another person be visible and point in his direction. Sitting with arms extended over backs of chairs and over people's shoulders is also considered inappropriate. So you see there are many ways for the sitting position to communicate respect or disrespect and disregard to others. Not knowing or not observing the proper etiquette could lead to poor business relationships and outcomes.

Finally, we come to an item that puts pressure on many people in business, creating problems and embarrassing situations. It is the acts of eating and drinking in public events. Even though different countries have different customs and habits, most business people try to follow the most common international table etiquette. Dining etiquette defines the following areas:

- Who sits first.
- Who is served first.
- How to hold and use the utensils.
- Which utensil to use and when, for which foods.
- Whether one can touch the food or any serving item, and whether one can lick one's fingers.
- How to use napkins.
- How to position one's hands and elbows.
- Whether it is permissible to make noise while eating.
- Whether one may chew with one's mouth open.
- Whether it is permissible to burp.
- Whether one may speak with a mouth full of food.
- How big of a bite to take.
- How much to eat.
- How to hold the glass.
- What to drink.
- How much to drink.
- Who leaves the table first.
- How dinner is ended.

I don't intend to give a course on table manners and dining etiquette. However, it is important to understand the importance of this issue and the many ways one can sabotage one's chances to succeed in business interaction and relationships.

Using correct table manners shows how sensitive one is to other cultures and their habits. It also indicates how well traveled, refined, and presentable the individual is in public.

Consider this: when you invite someone to your house for dinner, you expect him or her to abide by the rules of your household and vice versa. It is exactly the same when you are dealing with different cultures and different countries. When you are on a business trip to a foreign country, you must, and I repeat, you must follow the customs and habits of that country, and I mean all types of customs, unless you are unable to do so due to limitations beyond your control, such as allergies to certain foods; disability (for example, you are unable to sit on the floor due to bad knees), or lack of practice (as in the case of using chopsticks). Don't hide the truth; be upfront about your limitations so that there is no misunderstanding or assumptions made by your hosts about your motives and opinions. However, it is important to show interest in learning and acquiring the knowledge from those you are with, residents of the country you are visiting. In some cultures, for example, it is acceptable to use your hands when eating. It is critical to know your limitations when ordering food. Don't order what you don't know how to eat in a public or in a professional setting. Play it safe. In other cultures, it is acceptable for sound to come from the mouth, even burping, when eating. Also, there is a difference between European and American table manners such as the way to hold utensils, the knife and fork; for example, the wrist, hand, and elbow positions on the table. In some cultures, no one will take the last piece of food from the serving plate. These are just a few of the differences to keep in mind to avoid unwanted results.

Some business professionals refuse to change for whatever reason, and the negative effects of this attitude on their careers and businesses are clear. On the other hand, many have picked up foreign ways of conduct and the results have been extremely positive for them and their businesses. A perfect example of this is how shoes are taken off when sitting in the private rooms of Japanese restaurants and how Western business people adopted this custom. Always be on the lookout to learn the ways of others. It shows your interest, respect, and openness to their ways, and facilitates the development and nurturing of the relationships.

The key here is not to judge, criticize or ridicule. You might be on the receiving end of such treatments one day.

The Wisdon in What I Learned

Respect Is the First Step on the Ladder of Success

Don't Do to Others What You Don't Want Done to You

Respect in Order to be Respected

Respect Not Only the People, But the Company As a Whole

Chapter Eleven

It's All About People

In my first position as a marketing engineer, I worked for a very qualified go-getter type of manager. It was my first full-fledged marketing position. There were new things to deal with and learn every day. Sometimes I got so overwhelmed that I used to get frustrated with it all. Even though my behavior sometimes was out of line, my manager did not give up on me. The manager and the rest of the team made a solid effort to guide me through the learning curve and showed faith in me as a person and in my abilities as a potential marketing professional.

I remember in one of the strategy sessions we used to have, after I had argued a point, my manager made a comment to me that turned everything around for me, in a positive way. He said to me, "It would be great if you could just once accept a positive criticism instead of arguing the point and getting defensive." Then I realized that neither he nor the rest of the group were out to get me. They were giving me chances to learn and succeed. They had forgiven mistakes and inexperience on my part because they believed in my potential to become an excellent marketing professional. I did change and learn. I did not let them down. Within a year, I was managing five out of the seven product lines the group was responsible for, generating over 70 percent of the group's revenue.

It's all about people! Nothing of any value or benefit to communities or society as a whole can be achieved without people, not a one-man show, but a group effort. The reason is that every person brings to the mix a certain skill, talent, ability, motivation, idea, opinion, view, intellect, intensity, and desire. When all these traits are put together, the outcome is greater and richer than the outcome of an individual effort. No business would have survived without the mix of talents and capabilities of its people.

Not everyone can be a businessman or a financial person, a laborer or an engineer. Therefore, every talent must be nurtured and mentored to raise it to the next level of excellence, the next level of contribution. This is why every entity, whether it is a business, a country, or a family, must accept and encourage "organized diversity," for there is strength in organized diversity. Diversity is a wonderful thing, but it must be appropriately channeled and organized. If diversity is not organized, it will lead to confusion, chaos, and eventually failure that will tear the fabric of any entity. It is like the colors of a rainbow. Unless these individual colors are banded together, they will only be individual color beams, nothing more. However, when these *different* beams of color are banded together, a beautiful rainbow is created that will have a soothing effect on people. Also, consider that rainbows appear after rain showers, when calmness comes about. The point is that beautiful results for a business entity are created when its employees are calm and band together, thus creating an environment that is calm, serene, peaceful, and beautiful. Calmness, serenity, and peacefulness come about when there is harmony, trust, confidence, security, fairness, integrity, care, and compassion. When all these characteristics are present, the ultimate outcome is a successful business entity, which conducts itself ethically and with the proper etiquette, a humanized company.

Therefore, it is important for all business people at all levels to be mindful of the events that occur in the workplace. Listen and hear, look and see, think and feel the pulse of the business environment. This pulse is that of the personnel who are running the business. If the beat of the pulse is irregular or one beat is missing, action must be taken to correct the situation and the correction will always relate to and begin with taking care of the employees. Put away the ego and pride, bury the resentments and anger, forgive and take the lid off all feelings of compassion and support and let them flow. You will create a flourishing business entity.

Just as the clouds, rain, and oceans create and feed each other, so does the business and its people. Figure 18 demonstrates how the business and its people need, feed, and shape one another. One cannot and will not survive without the other.

Figure 18 People and business protect and nurture one another.

Business ethics and etiquette are the web that connects the various parts of the organization and act as its nervous system. It is what creates the healthy whole from its parts. These parts are the people of the business with all their human factors in play, the positive and negative ones. If you can imagine that the people of a company are its genes, then the ethics and etiquette are the characteristics of these genes, the DNA. When a gene is defective, disease is born and begins to grow until the body is overcome. The same holds true for a company when its people are unhealthy and broken—the company will eventually collapse. So make sure the people of the business entity, the genes of the corporate body, are healthy through proper ethics and etiquette. This way you will ensure the growth and prosperity for the business because *Business Is The People and People Are The Business.*

The Wisdom in What I Learned

Life Is Lived Through Choices and Decisions

Respect Not Only the People, But the Company As a Whole

Business Is The People And People Are The Business, Protect One and the Other Will Prosper

Figures

Index

Key Points Index

Notes

978-0-595-38297-2
0-595-38297-5

Printed in the United States
53199LVS00003B/124-144